Falling in Love with the Church is a much needed message for Hispanic leaders everywhere. I am thrilled that New Church Specialties is committed to servicing Hispanic church leaders with their teaching and services. We at AMEN are very happy with the growing relationship we have with them. Together we must speak a language of love.

Dr. Jesse Miranda, National Hispanic Leader
President, AMEN Ministries

What has deeply impressed me about New Church Specialties is the way the training they offer to church leaders is saturated with God's Word. Not only is the training practical and principle-driven, it is always delivered in a spirit which encourages personal, spiritual renewal. As he addresses the subjects of church health and church multiplication, you will find Larry McKain's writing filled with clear, practical strategies that are totally immersed in Scripture.

Dr. Keith Wright, District Superintendent
Kansas City District Church of the Nazarene

Dr. Larry McKain is passionate, articulate, and proven effective by the test of time. His latest book comes in a day of relentless change. McKain not only informs us how to meet the challenge but also how to optimistically embrace it and make it an open door for progress in carrying out the Great Commission. He also lays out a compelling contemporary rationale for the essential need to perpetuate effective denominations. The author provides the needed message for all who understand the urgent necessity to grow healthy churches.

Dr. Paul Cunningham, General Superintendent
Church of the Nazarene

At a time when many have given up on the church, Larry McKain takes us back to square one—loving the church as Christ does. In this book, he so refreshes our love for and devotion to the church that you will want to become involved in this effort yourself while you team with others to launch new churches. And if enough catch this love, we will experience a revival all across North America.

Dr. Aubrey Malphurs, Professor-Dallas Seminary
President-The Malphurs Group

When denomination-bashing is so common among evangelicals, it is enormously refreshing to hear someone stand up for the powerful, positive role interdependence plays among Christians and local churches. Larry McKain demonstrates that kind of courage and insight. He speaks with integrity as one whose personal journey has involved moving past the reality of organizational flaws, overcoming interpersonal hurts and experiencing personal and corporate sanctification. His love affair with the Bride of Christ is an example of a transformed outlook that reflects seasoned discipleship. His book is full of practical ecclesiology that will help coach you toward greater ministry effectiveness.

Dr. Jerry Pence
General Superintendent
The Wesleyan Church

Having attended a New Church University training event, I experienced first hand Larry McKain's passion for the Church and its mission in the world. In reading this book, I discovered the same passion and focus. The emphasis on loving the church, warts and all, is a corrective to the over-zealous individualism of our era. This is a must-read.

Bishop David G. Mullen, Sierra Pacific Synod
Evangelical Lutheran Church of America

Passion for the Church is in short supply these days. Many are enamored with technique but short on loyalty and love. Through personal narratives and the Scripture's witness, Larry McKain establishes the Church as the seedbed for the work of God in us all. Martin Luther seconds Larry's motion and emotion when he reverberates, "God is my Father and the Church is my Mother." Reading this book causes me to remember the joy that I first felt when I became a part of the Body of Christ.

Dr. Barry K. Carpenter
Director of New Church & Congregational Development
Kentucky Conference of the United Methodist Church

Dr. McKain practices what he preaches, having personally planted four churches and now training hundreds of church planters through New Church University. His next step has been the study of church planting and church health movements. In an age where independent attitudes and division have impacted both denominational families and informal church fellowships, this book is a fresh call to the link between biblical unity and church planting movements.

Dr. Jim Garlow, Author of *Cracking Da Vinci's Code*
Pastor – Skyline Wesleyan Church

Larry McKain's passion for seeing people come to faith in Christ is contagious. It is especially refreshing that he begins his discussion with a theology of the Church. His love for the Church shines through in all he writes. Dr. McKain challenges the Church not only to fulfill its call to mission, but also to be the people of God in healthy and holy relationships. *Falling in Love with the Church* is a timely book that pastors and church leaders will find to be full of insight and practical instruction.

Dr. Ron Benefiel, President
Nazarene Theological Seminary

Dr. Larry McKain & New Church Specialties provides the most effective seminars on church and ministry I know of. In their work with us, everyone who attended highly motivated to go back home and get to work on leading their churches to health and growth."

Bishop Ocie Booker, First Jurisdiction of Illinois
Church of God in Christ

We have really enjoyed our relationship with NCS Senior Consultants, especially Dr. Charles Lake. We have selected his materials for our Discipleship training and look forward to an exciting partnership with NCS in the days ahead.

Major Jan Sjogren, Evangelism & Corps Growth Secretary
The Salvation Army, Central Territory Headquarters

Larry McKain speaks from experience about the importance of starting new churches within a larger family of believers. He has started churches and consulted with and taught hundreds of others about starting new churches the right way. *Falling in Love with the Church* is an appeal for commitment to core values with a global mission. He shows from experience that local congregations are more effective in mission at home and abroad when they are partners in the Gospel with others.

Dr. Tom Nees, USA/Canada Mission/Evangelism Director
Church of the Nazarene

Dr. Larry McKain has become a great friend and a valued partner in ministry. His teaching on *Falling in Love with the Church* inspired and helped our pastors at our leadership conference recently as Larry presented a wonderful balance between right hearts and effective strategies. A caring and insightful Christian leader, Larry has—with both truth and grace—assisted us in crafting re-focus/re-start plans for several of our churches. Our movement is better and our ministry stronger because of our association with Larry McKain. It is great to see his heart now in written form.

Dr. John P. Williams, Jr., General Superintendent
Evangelical Friends Church

Dr. Larry McKain paints a gripping picture of God's mighty transforming movement. In candor, he shares how God closed the gap between his attitude and the attitude of Jesus toward the church. This book reminds us that we really do need each other *in and beyond* the local congregation. It will help create dramatic *agenda harmony* to launch God-glorifying church planting movements.

Dr. Jerry D. Porter, General Superintendent
Church of the Nazarene

If you work in the church, start churches, and care about the church, read this book. Larry McKain eloquently makes the case for falling in love with the church—or falling in love with the church again. If you have been hurt, disappointed, or disillusioned by your experiences, then you must read this book and find new hope for God's only plan to save the world. I plan to make it standard reading for all of our church planters.

Marcus Bigelow, President
Stadia New Church Strategies

Every pastor, young or old, will be greatly helped by reading *Falling In Love with the Church* by Larry McKain. Larry makes the case both for belonging to the church and for connectedness as well as I have ever read or heard. Part I is not only worth the price of the whole book, it is worthy of required reading for church membership!

Dr. Bill M. Sullivan
Retired Evangelism & Church Growth Director
Church of the Nazarene

Dr. Larry McKain brings to life the biblical relationships between Jesus, His followers and His Church. Jesus, who loved the Church and gave Himself up for the Church, is our model. A life spent loving the Church as Jesus loved the Church will be a life well invested—a life of great influence. This book will be of great benefit to all who read it.

Bishop Roger Haskins – for the Board of Bishops
Free Methodist Church

I want to recommend Larry McKain's book, Falling in Love with the Church. I heard Larry give a presentation on this subject and it so impacted me that I brought him in to Grove City Church of the Nazarene just to bless our congregation. Larry is right on target about what the church world needs to hear today. Every pastor and church leader will benefit from reading this book.

Dr. Bob Huffaker, Pastor/Church Consultant
Grove City, Ohio

Most pastors love their local church; a few have the capacity to love beyond their own denominational fellowship. In 30 years of church planting, I have not seen anyone with Larry McKain's passion for Christ's church at large. He possesses a powerful command presence, yet without arrogance. Giving help to plateaued churches as well as planters, the NCS system has arisen out of Larry's personal passion for the church. In print at last, these transferable concepts will provide the needed framework for both local and denominational renewal.

Phil Spry, Founder of Tellstart & Church Plant Strategies
Clayton, North Carolina

Jesus loved the visible, organized church of the first century and He loves His church today. This book challenges me to love her, to lead her gently and to live in her fellowship and community. We cannot serve the present age without a vibrant and living church—and the church thrives on love!

Dr. J.K. Warrick, Pastor—College Church
Olathe, Kansas

The reason we work with Dr. Larry McKain and New Church Specialties is because of the strong biblical foundation we see in everything they do. Dr. McKain has helped our denomination greatly, providing us with excellent organizational insights. His consulting with us has also helped us to realize the kind of questions we must both ask and answer if we are to position ourselves for effective ministry in the 21st century. I am happy these principles are now in print and available for all our people to read.

Bishop Emery Lindsay, President
Church of Christ (Hol) USA

Falling in Love with the Church is a book that reflects the practical skills and leadership attributes of Larry McKain. The book offers a comprehensive approach to a healthy, multiplication ministry and is a must read for every church leader in America. I plan to recommend it to all attendees at my seminars.

Dr. Stan Toler, Author and Speaker
Oklahoma City, Oklahoma

FALLING
in love
WITH THE
CHURCH

Building
Agenda Harmony
for Church Health
and Church
Multiplication
Movements

LARRY McKAIN

NCS PUBLISHING

I dedicate this book to the unsung, front-line heroes of the NewStart, ReStart, ReFocusing and Parent church movement, sacrificial clergy & lay leaders who unselfishly give themselves week by week for the vision of Christ's church. God knows each of you by name (Exo 33:17) and "He will not forget your work and the love you have shown Him as you have helped His people and continue to help them" (Heb 6:10).

I also dedicate this book to the staff team of New Church Specialties who have joined with me to serve the mission and ministry of Christ's church. It has been a wonderful journey together.
You are loved.

Acknowledgements

Every time I take a moment and reflect on the journey the Lord has all of us on, I am reminded that ministry is fully the result of the dozens of mentors God gives us along the way. For me, the list includes my parents, Marvin and Jo McKain who modeled love for the church in their everyday lifestyle; pastors I knew growing up like Dr. Crawford Howe; college and seminary professors like Dr. Larry Fine, Dr. Chic Shaver, Dr. Mendall Taylor and Dr. Ralph Earle; denominational supervisors like Dr. Forrest Whitlatch, Dr. Reeford Chaney, Dr. Charles Thompson and Dr. Keith Wright, who gave me opportunities to serve God's church, as well as exhibiting "great patience and careful instruction" (2 Tim 2:4) as they supervised me. It also includes great churchmen God used like Dr. Raymond Hurn, Dr. Paul Cunningham and Dr. Bill Sullivan, who all modeled before me great commitment to Christ's church.

Some of my mentors were lay people, men and women in local churches, too numerous to mention, but the lessons they taught were priceless. Some mentors came by way of books and tapes, people like Rick Warren, Bill Hybels, John Maxwell, Max Lucado and others. In the early 1990's, Bob Logan built and delivered the first Church Planter's Toolkit and coaching resources which helped me grow. Another exceedingly great mentor is John Wesley, whose life has influenced me greatly. He has passed on, but through his writings, "by faith he still speaks" (Heb 11:4).

A special thanks goes to Walt and Sharlyn Dixon, whose visionary support was crucial to the beginning of NCS. Words also cannot describe the joy I feel in being able to work with the tremendous New Church Specialties team God has brought together—our Board of Directors, Marvin McKain (an incredible Chief Financial Officer who serves so capably for $1 a year); Senior Consultants: Lonnie Bullock, Bud Bennett, David Bennett, Larry Cook, Dr. Dan Croy, Tim Gates, Dr. Ron Greeno, Dr. Bob Huffaker, Joel Hutchison, Joe Knight, Bishop Lindsay Jones, Simon Kiruris, Dr Charles Lake, Phil Stevenson, Dr. Fletcher Tink & Dr. Keith Wright; NCS Support Staff: Jolyne Bartley, Karen Bullock, Darla Elliott, Denise McKain and a host of other part-time staff who serve as coaches, help with NCU, etc. As I reflect on the adventure we are on together, my heart is full for the privilege of locking arms in ministry with each of you.

Finally, a huge debt of gratitude goes to my wife Denise. It has been her love, faithfulness and unselfish support these past twenty-five years that has made the journey a wonderful joy. I love you, Denise. Thank you for your heart of compassion for the poor and less fortunate, your giving spirit and everything you do every day for God, the church and our family.

Contents

Falling in Love with the Church is available in Spanish. All of the notebooks and power points used at New Church University have also been translated into Spanish and through our national partnerships, NCS now delivers Hispanic church leader training. For more information, call the NCS Main Office (816)746-6468 or e-mail us at KCOffice@NewChurchSpecialties.org.

To order copies of Falling in Love with the Church in either English or Spanish, visit us on-line at NCS Resources, www.NewChurchSpecialties.org, call (317) 881-3693, or write to us at:

NCS RESOURCES
& Growth Ministries
3490 W. Smith Valley Road
Greenwood, Indiana   46142

Introduction
God Is at Work!

"So I prophesied as He commanded me,
and breath entered them; they came to life
and stood up on their feet—a vast army."
Ezekiel 37:10

In our day, I hear the sounds of a new army coming! The sounds are not that of a congregation that continues to "do church" as they have always done before. The sounds I hear are the marching of those who hear the beat of a different drum. They are the innovators, the risk-takers, the ones who are anxious for adventure. They know they are called, spiritually gifted and led by God. They include both clergy and lay leaders. They are a growing group of new people within a new movement. They are a new army of NewStart, ReStart, ReFocusing, Parent church leaders and the judicatory leaders who serve them.

The leaders in this new army are different from the ordinary. In many ways, they are a breed apart. They do not come a dime a dozen, but they are a growing group of people critical to the long-term health and multiplication of Christ's church. They have a certain mix of spiritual gifts that God has uniquely endowed them with, in order to multiply the entry points into the Kingdom of Christ[1] through planting, refocusing, parenting and creating the climate where church health and church multiplication movements can happen.

Discontented with status quo and ordinary church routine, they feel the same urge as was felt in the heart of the apostle Paul. "It has always been my ambition to preach the gospel where Christ was not known, so that I would not be building on someone else's foundation" (Rom 15:20). When planting, refocusing or parenting a church, the same motivation as the apostle Paul is present—to reach people who do not know Christ.

Another characteristic of this new army is that they understand their work often goes unnoticed. When the gospel made its greatest advance in the book of Acts, non-Jews (men from Cyprus and Cyrene) went to Antioch and spoke to Greeks about Jesus (Acts 11:20). We have all heard about Paul and Barnabas being sent as the first church planting leaders from Antioch (Acts 13:2-3). Antioch was the first Parent church in the New Testament and launched the church planting movement of the Christian faith. But have you ever considered who started the Antioch church? From the Bible, we do not even know their names. But we do know "the Lord's hand was with them and a great number of people in Antioch believed," so Jerusalem headquarters

> There is a new army God is raising up of NewStart, ReStart, ReFocusing and Parent church leaders.

sent Barnabas down to find out what was going on (Acts 11:21-22).

Where church health and church multiplication movements happen, there are always scores of unnamed people working behind the scenes. They get little credit or recognition for their labor. But when they get to heaven, they will hear our Savior say, "Well done, good and faithful servant" (Matt 25:21). For them, that is enough because their ultimate purpose in life is to bring glory to God, not themselves.

Whether we are speaking one on one or reading a book by someone, after we spend time with a person and understand their thinking, we discover their attitudes, their spirit and their heart. Paul instructs us, "So…whatever you do, do it all for the glory of God" (1 Cor 10:31). God created everything to reflect His glory. "The heavens declare the glory of God; the skies proclaim the work of His hands" (Psa 19:1). When any person lives for his or her own glory, they sin. Paul wrote, "for all have sinned and fall short of the glory of God" (Rom 3:23).

Seeking our own glory rather than God's glory so easily happens, even to leaders in God's church. It occurs when our desire to be noticed or recognized becomes stronger than our passion to bring glory to God. We are "kept from willful sins, blameless and innocent" (Psa 19:13) when we "fan into flame" (1 Tim 1:6) our passion for God alone to be glorified.

Jesus' great desire was to bring glory to God. The night before Jesus died, He prayed to His Father, "I have brought you glory on earth by completing the work you gave me to do" (John 17:4). Paul thunders this focus when he writes, "Now to Him who is able to do immeasurably more than all we ask or imagine…to Him be glory in the church and in Christ Jesus throughout all generations, for ever and ever! Amen" (Eph 3:20-21). In our work as NewStart, ReStart, ReFocusing, Parent church, judicatory and denominational leaders, we must remember it is all about God, not us. The ultimate purpose of life and the church is to bring glory to God!

> The ultimate purpose of life and the church is to bring glory to God.

This is a book about church health and church multiplication. We will talk often about judicatories and fellowships, so let me define what we mean.

Judicatory: a generic term used to describe the organizational structures in various denominations, (i.e. conferences, districts, synods, presbyteries, conventions, dioceses, associations, regions, etc.) While church polity differs among denominational families, all denominations are made up of a collection of judicatories.

Fellowship: a term used to describe the hundreds of informal, non-denominational church groups that are tied together in mission through relationships rather than through church polity.

Church health and church multiplication are a

high priority for numerous judicatories, denominations and fellowships across North America. Numerous books on church health strategy and structure have been written. A large number of programs highlighting starting new churches, restarting churches, refocusing local congregations and parenting new churches have now been developed. These are new church "specialties" that have emerged as the church continues to find better ways of achieving God's mission in the world.

We must provide high-quality, specialized training for church leaders who are given these specialized assignments. The premise of this book, however, is that to accomplish all of this, to achieve church health and church multiplication within judicatories, denominations and fellowships, we need more than specialized training. We must take a different approach.

Any church health and church multiplication movement that is launched within a judicatory or fellowship requires church leaders to work closely together. The desire for a movement to happen, the resources needed and the right climate being created among existing churches are all important. How this can be achieved is the critical issue we must address.

We have learned that everything begins with how a judicatory or fellowship thinks and what it collectively believes about the church. Many North American Christians and even Christian leaders operate with a biblically fuzzy understanding of the church. Many do not love the church as Jesus loves it. We contend that for any church health and church multiplication movement to be launched and sustained long-term, a different approach must be taken. It begins with clear teaching about the nature of the church.

> We contend that church health and church multiplication movements require a different approach. It begins with clear teaching about the nature of the church.

God is glorified and His mission in the world advances greatly when groups of Christians lock arms together in His name to do the work of expanding His church. When God's church enjoys unity and agenda harmony, she is unstoppable! David writes, "How good and pleasant it is when kindred live together in unity" (Psa 133:1, NRSV). "For there the Lord bestows His blessing, even life forevermore" (Psa 133:3). A key issue related to church health and the multiplication of the church is gaining agenda harmony. What is agenda harmony? Let me define what we mean by these two words.

Agenda: "an outline or plan of the things that must be done."

Harmony: "a unified arrangement of parts with a common focus."

Put together, agenda harmony occurs when the members of a local congregation, judicatory, denomination or fellowship work together for a common objective, with a common purpose, in a common spirit.

The apostle Paul knew the importance of agenda harmony within the church and wrote, "If you have any fellowship with the Spirit...then make my joy complete by being like-minded, having the same love, being one in spirit and purpose" (Phil 2:1-2). How good and pleasant it is when a local church, judicatory or fellowship has these four characteristics: 1) they are like-minded, 2) they have the same love, 3) they are one in spirit and 4) they are one in purpose.

We contend that this is not just a suggestion or an option to God. "The Lord can bestow His blessing, even everlasting life" (Psa 133:3), only where there is unity and agenda harmony. Only where people are one in spirit and have the same love will we see lost and broken people come to Christ. It is only as local churches, judicatories and fellowships are "brought to complete unity that the world will know" (John 17:23) Christ's church as He designed us to be. We do not contend for structural unity, but spiritual unity.[2]

For the sake of the church Jesus loves, we urge every church leader to "make every effort to keep the unity of the Spirit through the bond of peace" (Eph 4:2). Unity of the Spirit does not mean I operate in practical independence and do my own thing. The health and mission of God's church begin with my own local church. But at the same time, it is much bigger than my local church. What is at stake is the salvation of our planet. This is not just about ourselves. God says a combination of unity and agenda harmony is the only way a spiritual climate is created that will consistently lead numbers of people to faith and eternal life. Healthy church multiplication requires agenda harmony among local congregations and the judicatories or fellowships with which they are connected.

I desire the following four ideas to shape the spirit of this book: 1) God is at work raising up a new army of church leaders. 2) Much of their work goes unnoticed. 3) Their ultimate purpose is to bring glory to God. 4) Agenda harmony is required for God's blessings on a local church, judicatory, denomination or fellowship.

> God's mission begins with my local church but it is much bigger than that. What is at stake is the salvation of our planet.

Discussions about church health and church multiplication immediately lead us into a discussion of strategy. This book will deal with some key lessons we are learning about effective strategy. We need solid strategies for starting new churches, restarting churches, refocusing churches, and parenting new churches. But we are learning that no matter how good the strategy, it will never make its desired impact unless we gain agenda harmony.

A healthy new church, restarted church, refocused church or parent church is never the result unless the leaders of that church are able to gain agenda harmony. Gaining biblical agenda harmony is where most local church and judicatory leaders fail. Great agenda harmony is never gained by using strategy. It is only gained by using and applying scripture. It is gained through the work of the Holy Spirit who creates and sustains the church. It requires people to have a clear spiritual understanding of the church. Church leaders must always remember that the power and spiritual results we need to do God's work never have their foundation in strategy, as important as it is. Spiritual power and spiritual results come through the Holy Spirit and the use of scripture. It is scripture, not strategy, which softens people's hearts, builds agenda harmony and brings transformation in people's lives.

> Healthy church multiplication requires agenda harmony among local congregations and the judicatories or fellowships with which they are connected.

This book has been laid out in four parts. We talk in part one about the biblical and practical foundations of a church health and church multiplication movement. What we believe greatly impacts how we behave. Part two details the lessons we are learning as we assist the launching and sustaining of church health and church multiplication movements. Part three describes the particulars of Integrated, Healthy Church Multiplication and the reality that it is not just one thing, but the building of healthy systems that leads to local church, judicatory and denominational health. Part four explains how we can fuel the church health and church multiplication movement where we serve.

My prayer is that after you read *Falling in Love with the Church*, you will learn to see and love the church as Jesus does. He literally "gave Himself up for her" (Eph 5:25). He expects us to do the same. Let us know what happens in your church health and church multiplication efforts. Drop us an email with the story of what God does through you at KCOffice@NewChurchSpecialties.org. Our

> Great agenda harmony is never gained by using strategy. It is only gained by using and applying Scripture.

desire is that God will take these pages and use them for the health and multiplication of His church, "until the earth is filled with the knowledge of the glory of the Lord, as the waters cover the sea," (Hab 2:14) and "the kingdom of the world has become the kingdom of our Lord and of His Christ, and He reigns for ever and ever" (Rev 11:15). Our prayers are with you.

Larry McKain, Executive Director
New Church Specialties

Part One

Biblical & Practical Foundations

1

Changing the Way We Think

"Christ loved the church and gave Himself up for her to make her holy, cleansing her by the washing with water through the Word, and to present her to Himself as a radiant church, without stain or wrinkle or any other blemish, but holy and blameless."
Ephesians 5:25-27

"I am the first to see her when she appears...she snaps heads sideward with every row she passes. That's the way it is with the bride. She remains hidden from friends and relatives...until the playing of the four-measure fanfare of Wagner's Wedding March. Then the notes of the fanfare sound. She steps out in view of all of us...Row by row, people turn to face the center aisle. They gasp, they cry, they laugh, they beam, they rejoice. The bride stands us on our heads. She is the center of the wedding and radiates every hope and dream on that day. Maybe that's why God chose the symbol of the Bride to represent the church. Christ meant for His church to turn heads..."[1]

We have all been to weddings. The first miracle that Jesus performed was at a wedding (John 2:1-11). In the Old Testament, God refers to the people of Israel as His Bride (Hos 2:19-20). In the New Testament, Paul likens the nature of the church to the marriage of a husband and wife: "the two will become one flesh. This is a profound mystery—but I am talking about Christ and the church" (Eph 5:32). In the final book of the Bible, John describes the greatest wedding of all time taking place at the Marriage Supper of the Lamb (Rev 19:6-9). The church is the Bride of Christ and will belong to Him for all eternity.

Paul Dramatically Changed His Attitude

Kevin Meyers is a NewStart church planter in Hilliard, Ohio. I will never forget how my heart burned as Jesus used him to open the following scriptures to me (Luke 24:32). They deal with the biblical and very practical issue of loving the church even when she is imperfect. Following the death of Stephen and before the conversion of Saul, persecution was great against the church. "All the believers except the apostles were scattered throughout Judea and Samaria" (Acts 8:1). The Bible says that "Saul began to destroy the church. Going from house to house, he dragged off men and women and put them in prison" (Acts 8:3). But on the road to Damascus, all that changed when Saul had a divine moment with God. A light from heaven flashed and a voice spoke, "Saul, Saul, why do you persecute me?...I am Jesus, whom you are persecuting" (Acts 9:4-5).

Do you see the inescapable link? The Bible says that Saul was persecuting *the church* (Acts 8:3). He was trying to destroy *the church*. But in Acts chapter 9, Jesus makes clear that Saul is not just persecuting an imperfect group of people. When he speaks badly of, when he hurts with his words or actions, when his attitudes toward the church are wrong, he hears a voice say, "I am Jesus whom you are persecuting." The teaching of the Bible here is clear. Any wrong I do to the church, in God's eyes I do to Jesus. This same persecutor

> Any wrong I do to the church, in God's eyes, I do to Jesus!

later writes, "This is a profound mystery, but Christ and His church have become one flesh" (Eph 5:30-31). What an attitude change he had! When he really met Jesus, Paul dramatically changed his attitude toward the church.

As a church leader, you have no doubt heard stories about people not following Christ fully in their lives because of their criticism of Christ's church. Just as Paul did before he was converted, thousands of people have persecuted Jesus in ignorance when they have intentionally done things that harmed Christ's church. From the cross where He hung and died for their congregation, we can still hear Jesus whisper, "Father, forgive them, for they do not know what they are doing" (Luke 23:34). There are millions of people in North America today who say they love Jesus; however, they just cannot stand the imperfect people who make up the church. This is a book that, in part, has been written to deal with this heresy. I wish I could report to you that this all-pervasive attitude of apathy and criticism toward the church is only found outside God's family. But sad to say, it is not. As I have traveled across North America, I have found that many people within the church have the same incorrect attitudes as the people outside God's family have. They love Jesus, but at best they tolerate the church. In their thinking, because of its imperfections, it is too much of a spiritual stretch for them to love it.

> When he really met Jesus, Paul dramatically changed his attitude toward the church.

As a Christian, I do not have the luxury of deciding the attitudes I will or will not keep. When I read something in the Word of God that challenges my attitudes or thinking, I cannot ignore it. I am not given the option of rationalizing my attitudes away by looking at someone else and saying, "I may not be perfect, but I sure am a lot better than him or her." Christlikeness is the standard by which we are all measured. "Jesus left us an example, that we should follow in His steps" (1 Pet 2:21).

There is no teaching more important for church health than a correct, biblical and practical understanding of the church. We have studied Willowcreek, Saddleback and numerous other churches where the Holy Spirit is at work transforming people's lives. All of these churches differ greatly in church polity, theological beliefs, strategy and structure. But they all have one thing in common. They are filled with people who love the church and are giving themselves up for the church.

They are following the example of Jesus when it comes to their attitude and practical belief about His church. God has given us clear teaching in His Word. These God-inspired ideas from Holy Scripture should deeply affect the way you and I think about the church.

> Many people within the church love Jesus, but at best, they tolerate the church.

The Huge Impact of Our Thinking

How we think makes a big difference. It makes all the difference in the world and in the world to come. How we think is not so much what we say, but really shows more what we are. What we ultimately become is determined by how we think. There is a little saying that clearly describes how we become what we are.

> Sow a thought, reap an act.
> Sow an act, reap a habit.
> Sow a habit, reap a character.
> Sow a character, reap a destiny.

How we think leads to how we act. How we act determines the habits we form. The habits we form determine the character we possess. Our character determines our destiny. This is not only true of individuals; this is true of local churches and fellowships. This is true of judicatories and even entire denominations. How we think makes a *huge* difference. In our local church, fellowship or judicatory, we are all a product of how we think. If the wonderful church you and I are part of is to be all that God has dreamed for her to be, it will begin with us and the way we think.

> What we ultimately become is determined by how we think.

If you and I are to be used in our generation to help the church be what Jesus gave Himself up for her to be, we must learn to think the way Jesus thinks. We must see lost people the way Jesus sees lost people (Luke 15:1-32). We must act the way Jesus would act, if He were leading the church in our skin. Because He is. We are His body, His flesh in the world today (1 Cor 12:27). As His church, we are given the incredible promise that it is possible for us to have "the mind of Christ" (1 Cor 2:16).

Terms and Definitions

In this book you will read the words NewStart, ReStart, ReFocusing and Parenting. Let me define what we mean by those words:

NewStart: the start of a new church—Anglo, ethnic or multi-cultural.

ReStart: the start of a new church with the use of a former building and/or remnant group of people. The judicatory or denomination may be involved, the former church leadership team is dissolved, and a new leadership team is formed by the ReStart church planter. It then operates much like a NewStart.

ReFocusing: the process of recapturing the vision and heart of Jesus for His church to be radiant, healthy and multiplying. This requires moving the church from an "inward" to an "outward" focus.

Parenting: taking personal ownership of a NewStart or ReStart project to multiply the Kingdom. It may involve one church or a group of churches coming together.

This is a book written for church leaders, both lay and clergy, about church health and church multiplication. The two are so intertwined that one cannot exist without the other. Any local church that focuses solely on its own health without keeping the church multiplication and global mission of Christ in view is in disobedience to the Head of the church. Judicatories and denominations that do not focus on church health but only on church multiplication and our global mission are short-sighted and self-centered. A vibrant church health *and* church multiplication movement within their region of responsibility should be the goal of all judicatory leaders.

> Church health and church multiplication are so intertwined that one cannot exist without the other.

Such a movement only happens when lay leaders, pastors and judicatory leaders experience agenda harmony around a shared vision for this kind of movement to take place.

Agenda Harmony with Jesus

Jesus was the greatest leader who ever lived. His coming to earth cut our calendar in two. Every time you and I write a check, we are reminded of how many years it has been since God entered the bloodstream of humanity.

> Never underestimate the power of God-inspired thoughts and ideas.

Jesus changed the world with shared thoughts and inspired ideas. Through the power of the Holy Spirit, the movement of Christianity erupted and that movement has impacted your life. Jesus had a vision for His church. He gave Himself up for the church and what she could be. He changed the world with teaching—with thoughts and ideas that came from God. He said, "For I did not speak of my own accord, but the Father who sent me commanded me what to say and how to say it" (John 12:49).

Never underestimate the power of God-inspired thoughts and ideas. This is why the teaching and preaching that occurs in your church every week has so much potential! God uses it to literally transform people's lives. Jesus died for your church. He carries it in His heart and mind. He says to you, "I know your deeds, your love and faith, your service and perseverance" (Rev 2:19). He has called you and me to join with Him as He builds His church (Matt 16:18).

To be more effective, we must learn better how to speak beyond our own ideas. We must have a deeper sense that the Father is telling us both what to say and how to say it to the church we love and serve.

You will notice in this book we use a lot of scripture. This is because large parts of this book have come from both prayer and insights from God's Word. Remember, great agenda harmony is never gained simply by using strategy. It is only gained by using and applying scripture. In my own life, when I hit a wall or face personal obstacles that cause me to change, a key shift usually occurs when I change my way of thinking because of the impact of scripture. Positive change starts happening when I begin seeking agenda harmony with Jesus.

The more I mature in the Lord and seek to follow His agenda, the more often I find myself asking questions like, "What does Jesus think about this?" "How does He feel?" "What would Jesus do?" I find myself praying prayers like, "Lord, help me to cry over the things which make you cry, to laugh at the things which make you laugh, to have a heart for the things for which you have a heart." I want to think the way Jesus thinks, feel what He feels and cry over what He cries over.

> I want to think the way Jesus thinks, feel what He feels. I want my will to be guided by His will and my values to reflect His values.

I want my will to be guided by His will and my values to reflect His values. I want my spirit to be filled with His Spirit and my heart to be aligned with His heart. I want to learn how to think the way Jesus thinks. I want His agenda to be my agenda.

This kind of thinking shift has led me to the Bible. I wish I could tell you every decision I make these days consistently lives up to the ideals in the paragraph above. It does not, but my heart is there. Over time I feel that my mind is slowly being renewed. More and more I am less driven by what Larry thinks and more consistently guided by what Jesus thinks. Gaining agenda harmony with Jesus is a process. Paul describes it this way: "Do not conform any longer to the pattern of this world, but be transformed by the renewing of your mind. Then you will be able to test and approve what God's will is—His good, pleasing and perfect will" (Rom 12:2).

> If your heart is responsive, the movement has already begun where you live!

If the church we serve is to change for the better, as lay and clergy church leaders, it will always begin with you and me changing the way we think. It will require us letting God regularly renew our minds by His Word so that we will gain His agenda and come into harmony with the other church and judicatory leaders with whom we serve. The result we seek is to lock arms together and create the vision Jesus has for His church, being "like-minded, having the same love, being one in spirit and purpose" (Phil 2:2). Do you have any interest in being part of a movement like that? If your heart is responsive, the movement has already begun where you live.

2
What We Think About the Church

"At the center...Christ rules the church. The church, you see, is not peripheral to the world; the world is peripheral to the church."
Ephesians 1:22, Msg

Over the past several years, I have traveled hundreds of thousands of miles speaking to hundreds of churches. I love them all—rural and urban, large and small, rich and poor, highly educated or with just lots of common folks. In the whole world, there is nothing else quite like the church. What a marvelous creation of God! What an incredible design! What a divine strategy! God takes imperfect people all over the world who believe in Jesus and He gathers them into divine groups. These groups meet every week for prayer, teaching, encouragement and correction from His Word.

> The church—what a marvelous creation of God! What an incredible design! What a divine strategy!

They lock arms with each other to provide a witness to the world that they are one with Jesus and the Father (John 17:21-23).

If you are a typical Christian living in North America, you probably love Jesus a lot more than you love His church. One of the reasons I feel compelled to write this book is to help you recover a correct, practical doctrine of *ecclesiology*. If you are a lay leader, don't let the word *ecclesi-ology* scare you away. Let's break it down. *Ology* at the end of a word simply means "the study of." Let's look at a couple of examples. Take the word *theology*. The Greek word for God is *theos*. So theology is "the study of God." Take the word salvation. The Greek word for salvation is *soterios*. So *soteriology* is "the study of salvation."

> Millions of Christians have not learned nor have they been taught the attitudes they should have toward the church.

Now take the word church. The Greek word for church is *ecclesia*, which literally means "the called out ones," or "the assembled." We are called out of the world, assembling ourselves together (Heb 10:25) and regularly being changed by God's Word to be sent back into the world. Ecclesiology is the study of the church. The study of Christ (christology) and the study of the church (ecclesiology) are so interlocked that no Christian can be a true follower of Christ without the church.[1]

The sad truth is that literally millions of Christians have spent their entire lives attending church, serving within the church and relating to the church, but they have never gone through a biblical study of the church. They have not learned nor have they been taught the attitudes they should have toward the church. They do not have a good practical doctrine of the church. Paul instructs us, "Watch your life and doctrine closely. Persevere in them, because if you do, you will save both yourself and your hearers" (1 Tim 4:16).

In many Christian circles, the word "doctrine" has come to be a negative thing. Doctrine is thought of as "dogma," something that is rigid, that causes me to disagree with other Christians, that creates opportunities for intellectual debate. This was never the understanding of the apostle Paul. Doctrine was much more practical, because for him, doctrine was directly tied to a person's behavior. He warns young Timothy, "Watch your life and doctrine closely" because he knew that both of these would affect the behavior of the church dramatically.

How God Changes Our Behavior

Do you have anyone in your church whose behavior needs to change? Do you have anyone whose attitude or actions need adjusting? If you are either in a church plant or a refocusing church, you may have several dozen. If you are refocusing a judicatory, you may have several thousand. If you are charged with refocusing an entire denomination, you may have tens of thousands. So what do we do? We must begin with one basic premise—a change in behavior always flows out of a change in beliefs. People behave because of what they believe. How do we get people to believe differently? We do not. That is the Holy Spirit's job. We cannot change people's beliefs. But we can and do need to better understand how the Holy Spirit does it.

> A change in behavior always flows out of a change in beliefs.

As we watch the way the Holy Spirit transforms people, it seems clear that He regularly uses some spiritual resources or "spiritual tools." In one place Paul describes them literally as spiritual weapons. He writes, "The weapons we fight with are not the weapons of the world. On the contrary, they have divine power to demolish strongholds" (2 Cor 10:4). There are some churches that try to operate with worldly resources; they try to change people without spiritual tools, and the result is always harm and loss.

Paul seems to see a spiritual battle taking place between the forces of God and the forces of evil, *even in the lives of very good people.* Every time transformation takes place or a change of mind occurs, it is because the Holy Spirit is at work. It is what we call a divine moment, a "God moment." It is not something we do; it is something God alone does. As a lay, pastor or judicatory leader, have you considered the resources you have at your disposal? Have you considered the tools God uses to change both you and those around you?

Divine Moments Create a Healthy Church

In building a church "so expansive with energy that not even the gates of hell will be able to keep it out" (Matt 16:18, Msg), the New Testament seems to indicate there are several spiritual resources we can use. Let me mention at least five: 1) prayer, 2) the Word of God, 3) the Holy Spirit, 4) an individual believer living a life of integrity, and 5) the collective witness of the church. At times, one weapon or tool by itself does not seem enough to win the spiritual growth battle. But when we use all the weapons in our arsenal together, Satan's work is tied up and his influence is driven back (Matt 12:29). God can and does use multiple spiritual resources as He creates divine moments that cause growth in people's lives.

> A divine moment is a spiritual step of obedience a person takes, in response to the Holy Spirit's prompting.

You may be thinking, "What do you mean by 'divine moment?'" A divine moment is a spiritual step of obedience a person takes, in response to the Holy Spirit's prompting. It always involves a person somewhere along the process of moving from "pre-Christian" to becoming a "global disciple." The decision to begin attending church, saving faith becoming personal, a decision for baptism, becoming a self-feeding Christian, joining a Sunday School class or small group, desiring spiritual growth and accountability, joining the church, becoming a worshiper, experiencing and growing in sanctification, getting involved in the church, using spiritual gifts in meaningful ministry, becoming a tither, giving beyond the tithe to the mission of Christianity worldwide, engaging in personal witnessing, are all steps in this process.

How would you like to have a church filled with people taking these kinds of spiritual steps? Every one of the steps above is connected with a "divine moment," when a person takes a spiritual step of obedience. In the Great Commission Jesus instructs us to teach people within the church "to obey everything I have commanded you" (Matt 28:20). He says, "Whoever has my commands and obeys them, he is the one who loves me" (John 14:21).

> Healthy churches understand the spiritual steps of obedience, the *divine moments* they need from God.

The promise of Jesus is that for Christians who obey His commands, He and the Father will come to those believers and "make their home" with them (John 14:23). What an incredible promise for every church. Healthy churches understand these spiritual steps of obedience, the "divine moments" they need from God. They learn to pray specifically and expect these moments to happen. They plan church activities with a focus on creating a climate where God can talk to people about taking steps of obedience to become mature, global Christians.[2]

What kind of divine moments does your local church

need from God? What divine moments are needed in your judicatory? What divine moments are needed in your denomination or fellowship? Have you clearly identified them? Are you regularly and specifically praying for them to happen?

When Paul talks about our spiritual resources, he says they have incredible power to "demolish strongholds," and are needed *even in the lives of good people like you and me.* Within the church, he offers an additional insight when he writes about the process of "...taking captive people's thoughts to make them obedient to Christ" (2 Cor 10:5). Here we see it again—God is highly interested in the way we think. God uses the church to help people take spiritual steps and every step is connected to the development of spiritual thinking. This is the process the Holy Spirit uses to lead all of our thinking to become obedient to the thinking of Christ (1 Cor 2:16; Phil 2:5).

> God uses the church to help people take spiritual steps. Every step is connected to the development of spiritual thinking.

When a church has people who are taking these spiritual steps of obedience and is developing people who think spiritually, church health happens naturally. We can help create the climate, but God alone does the work (John 15:5). The health of local churches, judicatories and denominations is directly linked to the thinking and spiritual obedience of the individual Christians who comprise them. When we correctly teach and when people do what our Lord commands them to do within His church (Matt 28:20), church health is the natural result.

Emphasizing Church Health
Over Church Growth

In the last 35 years, there has been a lot of writing on the subject of church growth. Growing churches have been studied all over the world, to find out the characteristics and causes of their growth. Some of this focus has resulted in increased effectiveness and the spiritual growth of the church. But along with it has come significant criticism from people who feel that a study of "church growth" alone does not accurately reflect the spiritual emphasis the church needs.

As a result, as we enter the 21st century, there has been a shift in focus from church growth to church health. We believe Rick Warren is right when he states, "the key issue for churches in the twenty-first century will be church health, not church growth."[3]

This is a much-needed biblical emphasis. Both Jesus and Paul seemed very interested, not only in the quantity of the crowd, but also in the quality of individual spiritual obedience.

In his best-selling book, *Fresh Wind, Fresh Fire*, Jim Cymbala correctly warn us of the three things most church leaders think about when asked how their church is doing. They usually respond with an answer that includes something like this: "Attendance is about 150, we've just finished remodeling our building, and our cash income this year is going to be about $175,000." Cymbala writes, "Attendance, buildings and cash. A-B-C: The new holy trinity."[4]

While all of these things are important considerations for local, judicatory and denominational leaders, the problem we face is when these things capture our heart and become the focal point. We do not mean for it to happen, but when our attendance, buildings and cash become the focus of a pastor, a church board, a judicatory or a denomination, they begin replacing our hunger to experience divine moments from God. The church does not stop believing in God's work through divine moments. They just stop happening because they are no longer our primary focus. We do not depend on them taking place, because we can operate and corporately survive without them. Over time in numbers of local church and judicatory settings, our gatherings become no different than a secular business or social service agency. It is then appropriate to write Ichabod over the door of the church, for "the glory has departed" (1 Sam 4:21).

> Other things replace our hunger to experience divine moments from God. The church does not stop believing in divine moments; they just stop happening because they are no longer our focus.

Paul reminds all of us within the church that everything we build is one day going to be tested. "Each builder must choose with care how to build....the work of each builder will become visible...it will be revealed with fire, and the fire will test what sort of work each has done" (1 Cor 3:10, 13, NRSV). We have discovered there is no relationship between the size of a church and the health of a church. We can take you to churches with 50 people in attendance where divine moments are happening and spiritual steps of obedience are taking place. We can take you to churches with 350 or 1,350 in attendance where no divine moments are happening. The reverse can also be true. Churches running 1,350 or 350 can be filled with spiritual steps of obedience and churches with 50 in attendance can be a place where spiritual thinking is absent. There is no relationship between size and health.

> There is no relationship between the size of a church and the health of a church.

We need all sizes of churches. Some people like large churches and others like small ones. What we are committed to assist the development of are genuinely healthy churches, large and small, that cultivate spiritual thinking and maintain a focus on divine moments from God.

We do not want to repeat any mistakes made by the church growth movement—we should allow past lessons to inform our future decisions. One of the best church health tools available for use by local churches is Natural Church Development.[5] It has been used by literally dozens of denominations and tens of thousands of churches worldwide.

At New Church Specialties, we use Natural Church Development as a diagnostic tool in analyzing the health of local congregations, based on eight characteristics that healthy churches all seem to have in common. This tool has been developed globally and is highly effective regardless of culture, context, socio-economic setting, etc. It is a very useful resource for our local church and judicatory partners.

Maintaining Spiritual Dependence

While I strongly believe in the need to highlight church health, there is a concern I have. In this emphasis, *we must regularly communicate who it is that creates a healthy church.* If not careful, we can inadvertently imply to pastors and lay leaders that our work to improve our church health minimum factor—improving empowering leadership, gift-orientated ministry, spiritual passion, functional structures, inspiring worship,

> All of our human efforts are designed to create a healthy climate where God can do His work.

holistic small groups, need-orientated evangelism and loving relationships—is what creates church health. It is not. This is simply a description of a healthy church.

Our actions, our strategies, our planning, all of our human efforts are designed to create a healthy climate where God can do His work. Do we believe it is important to do our part? *Yes!* But we must never forget it is *God alone* who does the work of building a healthy church. *God alone* causes people to take spiritual steps of obedience, not us.

Paul understood this well when he wrote, "I planted the seed, Apollos watered it, but God made it grow. So neither he who plants nor he who waters is anything, but only God, who makes things grow" (1 Cor 3:6-7). None of our human efforts can create a healthy church. To think otherwise is heresy. We do not create church health by the planning we teach church leaders to do at New Church University or any other human effort. "We are simply God's fellow workers" in His church (1 Cor 3:9).

> None of our human efforts can create a healthy church. To think otherwise is heresy.

We must always make certain in our ministries that we keep Jesus in His rightful place. In everything we do, He is the One who must become greater, and "church health" must be seen in its proper place as being a means to an end, but not the end itself. John clearly understood himself as simply a tool in leading people to Christ. He said, "No one can receive anything except what has been given from heaven...He must increase, but I must decrease" (John 3:27, 30, NRSV).

In the 21st century, as pastors and judicatory leaders, we will have to become specialists in our field if we are going to be effective long-term. Hundreds of NewStart, ReStart, ReFocusing, Parenting and judicatory leaders are now becoming specialists as never before. For this we praise God. But as we continue to grow and improve, we must be careful never to confuse the means with the end. By itself, church health is never the end. It is only the means to the end, the collective result. The end objective of everything we do is to cooperate with the Holy Spirit in creating a climate where God comes, changes a person's thinking and leads him or her to take spiritual steps of obedience. These spiritual steps happen in divine moments. It is all the work of God! It is these divine moments that create a healthy church.

> By itself, church health is never the end. It is only the means to an end, the collective result.

3

I Love to Be Corrected by the Word of God

"All Scripture is God-breathed and is useful for teaching, rebuking, correcting and training in righteousness."
2 Timothy 3:16

Do you remember being corrected when you were a child? Did you love it? You probably did not. Left to ourselves, none of us loves to be corrected (Prov 29:19). The Bible has a lot to say about correction. It teaches in Proverbs that if we ignore correction, we will lead others astray (10:17), if we hate correction we are stupid (12:1), if we heed correction we will be honored (13:18) and we show prudence and good sense (15:5). Mockers resent correction and will not consult those who are wise (15:12). Whoever heeds correction gains understanding (15:32). Jeremiah went through some great difficulties in following God's will for his life. He certainly had the right attitude when he wrote,

> In your spiritual life in God's church, do you regularly seek to be corrected by God?

"I know, O Lord, that the way of human beings is not in their control, that mortals as they walk cannot direct their steps. *Correct me, O Lord...*" (Jer 10:23-24, NRSV). Let me ask you, "In your spiritual life in God's church, do you regularly seek to be corrected by God?" There is a direct relationship between spiritual maturity, church health and the attitude of being teachable. People who spiritually grow want to learn. They seek wisdom and desire to be corrected by God in any way that makes them wiser. Proverbs instructs us, "If you had responded to my rebuke, I (wisdom) would have poured out my heart to you and made my thoughts known to you" (1:23), "if you correct those who care about life...they'll love you for it!" (9:8, Msg), "Give instruction to the wise, and they will become wiser still; teach the righteous and they will gain in learning." (9:9, NRSV), "the wise in heart accept commands (10:8), "Fools are headstrong and do what they like; wise people take advice (12:15, Msg), "Pride only breeds quarrels, but wisdom is found in those who take advice" (13:10).

> There is a direct relationship between spiritual maturity, church health and the attitude of being teachable.

Jesus Teaches on Biblical Correction

Remember what Jesus teaches? He always keeps calling us to take personal steps of obedience (John 14:21), to go and make disciples of all nations (Matt 28:19), to follow His example of seeking the lost (Luke 15:1-10), to continually trust in the power of the Holy Spirit and to be regularly corrected by His Word (Matt 22:29).

Jesus was a master communicator, a master at using "one-liners." He could take a complex issue and, in a short statement, give a solution people would never forget. Here is one example. The Pharisees were laying plans to trap Jesus in what He said. They came to Him, filled with duplicity. "Teacher, we know that you are sincere, and teach the way of God in accordance with truth, and show deference to no one; for you do not regard people with partiality" (Matt 22:16, NRSV). It was obvious these people hated Jesus and wanted Him out of the way.

Here came the trick question, "Tell us then, what is your opinion? Is it right to pay taxes to Caesar or not?" (Matt 22:17). From a human standpoint, Jesus was in a no-win situation. Roman soldiers were standing on one side of the crowd. If Jesus told the people it was not right to pay taxes, the soldiers would be up in arms because their salaries were paid by those taxes. If Jesus said they should pay taxes, the people would be up in arms because they hated paying taxes to Rome.

> Jesus was a master communicator. He could take a complex issue and in a short statement, give a solution people would never forget.

How did Jesus communicate in this no-win situation? He did it with a one-line statement. He replied (in modern language), "Does anyone have a quarter?" He held it up to the crowd, pointing to the face on the front, "Whose picture is this?" When they replied, "Caesar's," Jesus gave a one-liner most Christians in North America have memorized: "Give to Caesar what is Caesar's, and to God what is God's" (Matt 22:21). As a master communicator, Jesus understood the power of God-inspired thoughts, stories and short statements.

You would think after watching what had just transpired, the Sadducees would realize Jesus was more than a match for them. But here they came trying to baffle Jesus with a story about a man who was married to a woman, and later died. His brother married the woman, and he also died. After three funerals, all I can say is that the fourth brother was crazy! After the sixth brother died, can you imagine the emotions of the seventh brother walking up the aisle?

> Jesus taught, "You are in error because you do not know the Scriptures or the power of God."

As the story goes, all seven married the woman and all seven brothers died. The question the Sadducees asked Jesus was: "In the resurrection, who gets the woman?" When Jesus heard this story (as a master communicator), He responded with a one-liner that should be etched in the memory of every Christian leader and never forgotten. It is the solution related to almost every issue involving church health and church multiplication. Jesus replied, "You are in error because you do not know the Scriptures or the power of God" (Matt 22:29).

I want to suggest that nearly every time the church has a problem, an error or the need for correction in some way, either we do not understand the Scriptures or we are not trusting the power of the Holy Spirit.

Every time the church is not healthy or the multiplication of God's church is being thwarted, it is because the church needs some kind of repentance and correction. This is what Jesus taught.

Maintaining an Openness to Change

Paul writes, "All Scripture is God-breathed and is useful for teaching, rebuking, *correcting* and training in righteousness" (2 Tim 3:16). As I attend church, one of the main purposes of the Bible is to regularly correct me. If I am a maturing Christian taking spiritual steps of obedience, it may not be easy. But every Sunday when I gather to worship, my attitude will be, "Lord, I want

> If I am a maturing Christian, I will have regular changes of mind and corresponding changes in my life.

to be corrected today by the Word of God. Would you teach me, guide me, reveal to me the changes you want me to make in my life today?"

As we work with churches in the ReFocusing process, we are finding a prerequisite to ReFocusing is repentance, brokenness and developing a sense of urgency to be different. "A broken spirit; a broken and contrite heart, O God, you will not despise" (Psa 51:17). Every maturing Christian taking spiritual steps of obedience will seek to be corrected as often as he or she can, by the word of God.

The Greek word for repent is "*metanoia*," which means "a change of mind and a corresponding change of life." It is not just blatant sinners outside God's church who need to repent and be corrected by God. If I am a maturing Christian taking spiritual steps of obedience, the Holy Spirit will regularly prompt my thinking to change. I will have regular changes of mind and corresponding changes in my life. I will never stop growing and maturing. I will never feel that I have spiritually arrived. God will continue showing me how I can take more steps toward becoming a global Christian who sees the world every day through the eyes of Jesus. I then will remain humble, broken and teachable before God. How many people like this would you like to have in your church?

> A prerequisite to ReFocusing is repentance, brokenness and the development of a sense of urgency to be different.

4
What the Church Is... and Can Be

"His intent was that now, through the church, the manifold wisdom of God should be made known..."
Ephesians 3:10

We need to approach the subject of what the church is and can be with a deep sense of awe and reverence. This is holy ground. We want God to correct our thinking about the church if in any way our thinking is not in line with His Word.

We must begin by examining the religious thought of much of the North American church as compared to the practical doctrine of the church taught in the New Testament.

Western culture has emphasized the freedom of the individual and his or her personal relationship with God. If this emphasis on the individual is not balanced with a correct teaching about Christian community, Christians will live with only partial truth.

> Partial truth ultimately leads to incorrect beliefs and spiritually immature behavior.

Partial truth ultimately leads to wrong thinking, incorrect beliefs and spiritually immature behavior. Sad to say, this spiritual problem is found all over North America, both inside and outside local congregations.

What is the Church?

What is the church? Let me offer a practical definition. "The visible church is an imperfect group of Christ-followers who have been gathered by the Holy Spirit, who assemble regularly for worship and the administration of the sacraments[1] and who seek correction from God's Word. These Christ-followers proclaim the gospel by locking arms with each other and providing a witness to their community and the world that they are one with Jesus and the Father (John 17:21-23). They cooperate with the wider church to fulfill Christ's global mission of making disciples of all nations."

I would never presume to suggest that in this brief paragraph we can summarize or clarify the volumes that have been written in the last two-thousand years about the church. But literally millions of North American Christians need solid teaching and correction on this issue. What we believe about the church is foundational to every church health and church multiplication movement.

Jesus Loves Imperfect Churches

As lay and clergy church leaders, we have all heard people make comments about the imperfections of the church. Many of the reasons people give for not participating in God's church flow out of a spirit of criticism. There are millions of people today who say they love Jesus; their problem is with the imperfect people who regularly attend church.

Our call as church leaders is to teach our generation it is God's will that they embrace, fall in love with, and give themselves up for the imperfect group of people Christ gave Himself up for—the church. Although Jesus and God are both perfect, the church, the physical expression of Jesus in the world today, is not perfect. We must teach this is not a surprise or a discouragement to God. He is always doing more underneath than we can see on the surface.

Jesus knew His church would be imperfect when He planted and regularly refocused the very first one in Jerusalem. If you feel like you have problems with your church, look at the problems Jesus dealt with.

1. The treasurer was stealing money from Him.
(John 12:6)
2. One of His key church leaders betrayed Him.
(Luke 22:47-48)
3. When He needed His leadership team, they slept.
(Matt 26:40)
4. When pressured, the leadership team deserted Him.
(Matt 26:55-56)
5. His closest key leader disowned Him.
(Matt 26:75)

Several encouraging truths stand out as we evaluate

the problems in the church with which Jesus worked. If your treasurer is not stealing from you, if you are not being betrayed by key leaders, if only half of your leadership team sleeps during meetings, if all your leaders are not deserting you and if your best supporter has not disowned you, you are doing better than Jesus did.

If you have seen the movie, *The Passion of the Christ*, replay the scenes in your mind again. The treasurer is stealing money, key leaders are betraying Jesus, His leadership team cannot stay awake, when His key leaders do wake up, they desert Him, and His closest supporter denies knowing Him with a string of curses. Here is the question. Would you go to the cross for that group of people? Would you give yourself up in sacrifice for this kind of church? Jesus did.

If these things happened to Jesus as a leader, we can certainly expect there will be many kinds of problems every church leader will have. Jesus also had a group of very imperfect people. Even though they hurt Him, Jesus gave Himself up for them. He gave Himself up for the church (Eph 5:25). He did this because He knew the only way local churches would become healthy all over the world, is for people to follow His example and give themselves up for their church.

A God-Chosen Institution

We have been taught in North America that salvation is an individual choice we make, but God's Word teaches that Jesus sacrificed Himself for more than just my individual sin. Jesus died for the church, for He realized that only when I as a Christian walk in harmony with God's church, can I be "made holy and blameless" by God's Word as I should (Eph 5:26). When I fall in love with the church, I am falling in love with the institution God has chosen to bring salvation to the world, and the vehicle He is using to prepare me to meet Him.

> When I fall in love with the church, I am falling in love with the institution God has chosen to bring salvation to the world and the vehicle He is using to prepare me to meet Him.

The church has and always will live in tension. She celebrates what God has done so far, but she also longs to be perfect like Christ. In this world, she is not perfect. She has "stains, wrinkles and blemishes" (Eph 5:27). Here is the vision of Jesus for your church. As your church is regularly washed with God's Word and the people within your church take spiritual steps of obedience, the church is able to move from the wrinkled stage to the radiant stage!

The Bible says, "His intent was that now, through the church, the manifold wisdom of God should be made known…" (Eph 3:10). God's intent is to make His wisdom and revelation known through your church and hundreds of thousands of other churches like it. There is no plan B. We are it. He has chosen to use us to bring His salvation to the planet.

The people the Holy Spirit has gathered in your church are not perfect and they never will be until they get to heaven. Jesus has a lot more "correcting" to do on them just as He does on you and me. Jesus loves your church and has a clear plan to make her holy as He cleanses her week by week with correct teaching from His Word (Eph 5:25-26).

Jesus in the Flesh

Paul says, "In the same way a husband and wife are 'one flesh,' I want to give you a profound mystery—Jesus and His church have become one flesh as well." Jesus is so committed to your church that He has united and become "one flesh" with her (Eph 5:32).

What does this mean in a practical sense? When you see Mary Lou (a widow) sitting on the third row, left side this Sunday morning, you are seeing Jesus in the flesh. When you see Mark and Becky sitting on the fifth row, right side this Sunday morning, you are seeing Jesus in the flesh. It is the Holy Spirit Himself who has drawn Mary Lou, Mark and Becky together within your church. Every week you gather, Jesus is among you! It is so important that you understand why He prayed for you the way He did before He went to the cross. (John 17:20-23). What your church is part of is so

> There is no plan B. We are it. God has chosen to use us to bring His salvation to the planet!

much larger and more incredible than what you visibly see every week. It is bigger than all of us. It is eternal!

How can you and I think more correctly about the church as we come to worship each week? You and I know many people who have been around the church all their lives, yet some of them may not act as spiritually mature as others who have been around the church just a few months. There is a big difference between growing old in the Lord and growing up in the Lord. Nowhere is this more apparent than in the way some Christians act in relationship to the visible church.

> What your church is part of is so much larger and more incredible than what you visibly see every week. It is bigger than all of us. It is eternal!

Fourteen Truths About the Visible Church

We choose to use the term "visible church" because many people in our culture want to identify with Jesus and the "invisible" church. They believe they can be good Christians and never attend church. They church hop and church shop but never stop. These professing Christians do great damage to Christ's church, especially as their actions become socially acceptable to larger numbers of people. Both Gallup and Barna Research polls reveal there are tens of millions of Americans who claim a personal faith in

Christ, but have no commitment to any visible church.

In the Bible, the word church is used two ways. First, it is used to refer to every Christian that has ever lived in time. This is the church "universal," and the word church is used this way in the Bible four times. The other 110 times it is used in the Bible, the word church refers to a visible, local body of believers. The church at Corinth, the church at Philippi, the church at Thessalonica—these were all visible, local bodies in which individual Christians were expected to become a vital part.

> God is the one who created the church. To say that I am a Christian and not regularly assemble with God's people is to deny what God has created and called me to be.

In early church teaching, it is inconceivable that someone could be a Christian and not be a vital part of a visible, local body of Christ. Dozens of commands given to Christians in the New Testament cannot be obeyed unless we are an active part of a visible church. Every week I attend worship, I need to regularly remind myself of the nature and purpose of the church. I am to love her. What follows is a list of fourteen things the Bible teaches us about the visible church.

1. The visible church is a divine community. God is the one who created the church. It is not a "Christian option." Every Christian should join and actively participate in a visible church. To say that I am a Christian and not regularly assemble with God's people is to deny what God has created and called me to be (Heb 10:25; Eph 1:4-23; 2:12-22; 1 Pet 2:9).

2. The visible church is where Christ is present and at work. "Where two or three are gathered in my name, there am I in the midst of them" (Matt 18:20). Healthy churches have a profound awareness of the Lord's presence as they gather each week. Large churches or small, when we come together in the name of Christ, Jesus is at work. Divine moments happen and spiritual steps of obedience are taken.

3. The visible church and Jesus were one at Pentecost. Through the outpouring of the Holy Spirit and spiritual presence of Jesus, the preaching and teaching of Jesus greatly multiplied through His followers. "They were truly one" (John 17:21) and the world came to

> If you are a Christian, you are to become a vital part of Christ's visible body and make it better. No cop outs allowed!

believe. From the beginning, the church and Jesus were never separated in any Christian's thinking. The great early church father Ignatius wrote, "Where Christ is, there is the church."[2]

4. The visible church and Jesus are still one today!
The actions of the church are and should be the actions of
Christ. What Jesus began while He was in the flesh, the
church now has taken on the responsibility to fulfill. He is
the Head of the church. We are His body in the world, His
hands, His feet, His voice, His heart. No one is perfect,
but if you are a Christian, you are to become a vital part
of His visible body and make it better (1 Cor 12:27). No
cop-outs allowed!

5. The visible church is what Jesus died for. Jesus did
not just die for individuals; He died for your church. He
"gave Himself up" (Eph 5:25) so your church could be
holy (Heb 12:12).

6. The visible church is what Jesus will return for. Jesus
will return for the believers from your church and they will
be joined together with Him for all eternity (Rev 19:7-9; 1
Thess 4:13-18).

7. The visible church will never be perfect in this life. The
church Jesus founded was full of imperfection. Paul wrote,
"but when perfection comes, the imperfect disappears...
Now we see but a poor reflection as in a mirror..." (1 Cor
13:10, 12). It is the calling of Christian leaders to offer
correct teaching so the church can move from wrinkled to
being radiant (Eph 5:27).

8. The visible church is where I spiritually mature in

Christlikeness. The church is the institution God has chosen to help prepare me for service to the world and the vehicle He is using to prepare me to meet Him. It is where I am regularly washed with the water of His Word and challenged to become more like Him.

9. The visible church is my spiritual family. Paul writes, "Let us do good to all people, especially those who belong to the family of believers" (Gal 6:10). Did you know that your spiritual family, the church, will last longer than your physical family? You will be in the family of the church forever.

> The church is where I am regularly washed with the water of God's Word and challenged to become more like Him.

10. The visible church is where I discover and use my spiritual gifts. "Now about spiritual gifts, brothers, I do not want you to be ignorant" (1 Cor 12:1). "Each one should use whatever gift he has received to serve others" (1 Pet 4:10). If I do not use my God-given spiritual gifts to help build up Christ's church, the church and Jesus' work in the world will not be what it could be. Every little part matters a lot (Eph 4:16).

11. The visible church is where I receive spiritual protection. The Bible commands pastors, "Guard....the flock, of which the Holy Spirit has made you overseers. Be shepherds of the church of God....because savage wolves will come in among you.... and distort the truth" (Acts 20:28-29). Part of the church and pastors' responsibility is to help the flock separate truth from error.

> If I do not use my God-given gifts to help build up Christ's church, the church and the work of Jesus in the world will not be what it could be. Every little part matters a lot.

12. The visible church provides me with spiritual accountability. The Bible says, "Brothers, if a man is trapped in some sin, you who are spiritual should restore him gently....Carry each other's burdens and in this way you will fulfill the law of Christ" (Gal 6:1-2). The reason numbers of people do not join a church is because they do not want to be held accountable for personal growth and change. This is a spiritual maturity and obedience issue.

13. The visible church helps me fulfill Christ's Great Commission. Every Christian is called to "make disciples of all nations" (Matt 28:19). Separate and isolated, I cannot be the global Christian I should be. It is by linking arms with the wider church, sending and supporting her missionaries, that I am privileged to actively participate in the church as a global movement.

14. The visible church has many "tribes" God is using today. Many different denominations adhere to the basic tenants of the Christian faith and are faithful to witness Jesus Christ as their Lord. Christians do not have to "see eye to eye" on every issue to be able to "walk hand in hand."

This is what the church is…and can be! The Head of the Church is calling you to become a vital part of His visible army. Do not be like the soldier who says, "I want to fight in the war. I just do not want to be a part of any specific platoon. I will fight wherever I want to, on my own." The Bible instructs us, "No one serving as a soldier gets involved in civilian affairs—he wants to please his commanding officer" (2 Tim 2:4).

> The visible church helps me fulfill Christ's Great Commission by linking arms with the wider church, enabling me to become a global Christian.

The Bible teaches that the church cannot operate with you remaining uninvolved in Christ's visible church; He expects you to enlist. The stakes are high. The battle lines are drawn. The community you live in, the extended area you are part of, and the world waits for your response. Will you sign up and show up for active duty in your local church? Eternal issues hang in the balance. Now is the time for you to say yes.

5
A Case for Connection

"Obey your leaders and submit to them,
for they are keeping watch over your souls and will
give an account. Let them do this with joy and not
with sighing—for that would be harmful to you."
Hebrews 13:17, NRSV

If you are an entrepreneurial church leader and part of a denominational family, the probability is high that at sometime in your life you have thought about "going independent." If you are part of a fellowship that has any kind of history or tradition, you have probably been tempted to separate yourself from it. I have spoken to dozens of strong, entrepreneurial church leaders in the past several years, and when I relay my experience on this subject, every one of them knows the feeling and can identify with the issues we are addressing here. Leaders with great potential are usually those who live on the edge, not those who "play it safe." Leaders with great potential usually reject the status quo and question "why we do what we do, the way we do it." If denominational leaders are prudent, they will learn how to wisely manage entrepreneurially-oriented leaders and leverage their abilities for the health and multiplication of the church.

Understanding Spiritual Legacy

It seems to me the best way to teach the subject of commitment to a denominational family or fellowship is simply share the lessons God has taught me on my own journey. I would encourage you sometime to do a study on the theme of spiritual heritage. We all have one. It may stretch down through several generations, or if you are a first generation Christian, your personal heritage within the church may be just beginning. David talks about this spiritual legacy we are given by those before us and writes, "God, you have given me the heritage of those who fear your name" (Psa 61:5).

> Denominational leaders must learn to wisely manage entrepreneurially-oriented young leaders and leverage their abilities for the health and multiplication of the church.

Spiritual legacy is built over time. It includes a large number of very typical Sundays. Many Sunday mornings seem to be no different than the previous week for the faithful who show up. When they arrive, worship and serve, they have no idea how their faithfulness will create a spiritual legacy. They do not know how their ordinary spiritual routine will touch a family, a generation, even future generations of Christians yet to be born.

They come together as a group of imperfect people who believe in Jesus. They gather regularly with each other in this "God-created" group called the church. They meet every week for prayer, teaching, encouragement and correction from God's Word. They lock arms with each other to provide a witness to their community and the world. Through their faithfulness to Christ across the years, they pour spiritual legacy into the life of every person who attends. The people who are touched carry the legacy with them to their graves. Even if the local church where they meet should ever close it doors in the future, the legacy never dies! This spiritual heritage the church offers to people has an eternal impact.

Dr. Bill Sullivan reminds us that every church currently in existence in North America started out as a church plant, offering a spiritual legacy. "Anytime anywhere people worship or serve in a church…they

> Even if a church closes its doors in the future, its spiritual legacy never dies!

benefit from the efforts of some church starter and core group who began their church. Every church…stands as a memorial to someone's vision, sacrifice and sweat. Some sold farms. Some quit jobs. Some went out under the sky to preach with no security…Someone paid a great price to begin your church. Never forget it. And everyone who has come to faith as a result of that church must feel a debt of gratitude to those selfless folks who started it. They were persons of amazing vision, tenacity and faith."[1]

How My Spiritual Legacy Began

I had the fortunate privilege of a great spiritual heritage given to me through a small country church in Kurtz, Indiana. The town of Kurtz has a population of only 125 people. The church began very small and has never really been large. There are literally tens of thousands of churches, connected with multiple denominations and fellowships all over North America that are just like the Kurtz church.

The Kurtz church was organized as a denominationally-connected church back in 1920. The church began out of a series of religious meetings just like thousands of other churches in America. A group of committed Christians traveled to Kurtz from Seymour, Indiana. They put up a tent and preached in the "Kurtz Grove" for several weeks as an outreach to people who were non-Christians or not active in a church. They held a membership class after the meeting was over and, according to church records, twelve people joined. If you believe the Bible's teaching, it was the Holy Spirit who drew those people together to form that small country church.

Back in her beginning, the Kurtz church did not have what she has today. There was no limestone parsonage, fine fellowship hall, padded pews or indoor plumbing. But what that small group of believers had when they came together was a sense of God's presence, the working of the Holy Spirit and a mission to lock arms and touch those outside the church with Christ's love. The faithful people in this country church showed up every Sunday morning for worship. They unlocked the doors, turned on the lights, rang the bell and prayed for unchurched people by name. For sixteen years they did that, and the church grew from twelve to sixty people in attendance.

It was a Sunday morning in the spring of 1936. Two young girls, ages two and one, were playing outside on their farm near Kurtz. Their father, a young farmer named David Whittredge, was plowing behind a team of horses out in his field that morning. It had been his custom to work on Sunday rather than attend church. He had not been raised in a Christian home. His father was an alcoholic, his parents were divorced when he was twelve, and he had moved to southern Indiana to live with his uncle. He met and married a school teacher who was also unchurched. Together they bought a farm outside of Kurtz. Spiritual influence in their lives did not exist until some people from this young church in Kurtz started to call on them. They invited David and his wife to worship. They urged him to consider raising his two girls in the church. They started praying for him regularly by name.

> They unlocked the doors, turned on the lights, rang the bell and prayed for the people. They had no idea how their faithfulness would create a spiritual legacy.

Plowing out in the field that morning David heard the church bell ring. He had heard it on Sundays before. But the people of the church had been praying. A divine moment happened. He suddenly had a change of mind, a change in his thinking! In answer to their prayers, he stopped plowing, took the team of horses back to the barn, went to the house and said to his wife Fern, "Get the girls ready. Today, we are going to visit that church." The morning he walked in, the Holy Spirit was present. Another divine moment happened. David Whittredge and his wife Fern committed their lives to Christ that morning.

You may be wondering why that morning in 1936 is so meaningful in my life. The one-year-old girl David and Fern took to church that day ultimately became my mother. Psalm 103:17 says, "But from everlasting to everlasting the Lord's love is with those who fear Him, and His righteousness is with their children's children." God used the church to touch my grandfather's life and his decision that day transformed future generations in our family.

In 1946, my dad's family began attending the Kurtz church. That is how he met my mother. In 1953, Fern was sustained by the church when David was killed in a tractor accident on the farm. I was born in 1956 into that country church. I have heard many stories from my relatives about my grandfather. Although I never met him physically, I have heard much about him spiritually. I am told he was a real leader of men, a man's man and a strong Christian lay leader. One thing I am told repeatedly is that he loved the church. After his conversion to Christ, he was zealous in encouraging others all over the county to attend. He became Sunday School Superintendent, and at one point the Kurtz church had an attendance of over 250 people. For seventeen years, he created a spiritual legacy that he passed on to me, though we never met.

If we had the time to research it and the venue to share it, every Christian reading this book could tell a similar story about the way God has used the imperfect, visible church to touch and transform your family. With every transformation, with every divine moment, spiritual legacy is formed. A spiritual heritage is established. It took me a number of years and some spiritual maturing to fully understand and appreciate this.

> With every life transformation, spiritual legacy is formed and spiritual heritage is established. It took me a number of years and some spiritual maturing to understand this.

Managing Entrepreneurial Church Leaders

When you have church leaders out on the edge in ministry, reaching new people for Jesus, experimenting with new approaches, testing the status quo, people who live by the letter of the denominational structure usually feel uncomfortable. At this point, judicatory leaders have a choice to make. When they create a flexible climate that not only allows but encourages entrepreneurial creativity in ministry, they thrive. If they choose to restrict and create a strong climate of control, they choose to die.

I am grateful God placed me in a denominational family that encourages entrepreneurial activity most of the time. However, numbers of denominations continue to need more training for judicatory leaders, helping them understand their role in managing church planters.

> When judicatories choose to create a flexible climate that encourages entrepreneurial creativity in ministry, they thrive.

Sometimes the greatest contribution a judicatory leader makes to healthy church multiplication is to act as a "heat shield" between the entrepreneurial leader and people from other established churches within the judicatory family.

I have a personal experience pertaining to this. The year was 1989. I was serving in our third church plant, was ahead of my time and greatly "stretching the envelope" for the judicatory of which I was a member. My wife and I had started the church with only two people besides our family. The Lord blessed, however, and the church was growing rapidly in an upper middle income community. We were 15 months into the project. We were worshiping in a school and had moved the church office out of our home into a multi-room office in a nearby business park. We had hired a full-time worship and administration pastor, a part-time office manager and from the first day had continued to give 10% of our income away to missions through our denominational family.

Our judicatory had given us a total of $13,800 to begin the church. The fact that we financially survived was a miracle in itself. Like many church planters understand, the level of energy and sacrifice to start a new church from the ground up with few resources is enormous.

At the same time, many of my pastoral peers within the judicatory viewed what we were doing with high degrees of suspicion. Our church was very different in style from a number of the other churches in the judicatory family.

Several pastors wrote letters to the judicatory leader complaining about our ministry and copies were sent to me to read. I wish I could tell you that I responded to these criticisms with a high degree of spiritual maturity. I am sorry to say, I did not. Looking back on it, I was a very difficult church planter to manage. Some of the decisions I made and the things I said to those in spiritual leadership over me were not filled with either wisdom or tact. Much of the conflict was the result of my own immaturity.

How God Taught Me to Love the Church

Even though I never spoke openly with our leadership team about the conflict, the people closest to me could sense my frustration. I will never forget the night that "the discussion" occurred. One of the men in the church was a builder who had helped my wife and I build a small new home, the very first one we had ever owned. We had just moved in and about ten people from the leadership team were meeting in our living room. With the exception of one, all of them had no previous background with the denomination that had sponsored us.

Sensing my frustration, a discussion ensued about our denominational connection. This was before the church was formally chartered and organized, so the only ties we had with the church were the ties I had personally. One of them finally asked, "Larry, why do you stay with your denomination? Is it the retirement program?" Another offered, "If you would like to consider going independent, we could gather the resources beginning tonight that would secure your retirement."

> Because I did not understand agenda harmony, a highly influential lay leader caused a church split and a group of people walked out the door with 40% of the church's income.

Because I did not fully understand agenda harmony, when we came down to organize as a denominationally connected church, a highly influential lay leader who did not want the connection caused a church split, and a group of people walked out the door with forty percent of the church's income. The attack by this group on my personal character was one of the most difficult things I have ever experienced. It caused a great deal of emotional pain for my wife Denise and our family.

I have learned so much about church planting over the last 25 years. God never wastes a hurt if we are willing to learn from it. People have asked me where I developed my understanding of the church and what motivated me to study what the Bible says about the church. They ask how I came to put this teaching on "Falling in Love with the Church" at the center of New Church University training. My response is always the same. When I came within a hair's breath of leaving my denominational family, when I was in pain and felt all alone,

> God never wastes a hurt if we are willing to learn from it.

at that point I was forced to study what it was I was willing to give my life up for. In my own pain I read passages like, "fix your eyes on Jesus...you have not yet resisted to the point of shedding your blood" (Heb 12:2,4). I read what Jesus went through with the church leadership team with whom He worked. I read how He was rejected and cursed and still "gave Himself up for the church" (Eph 5:25).

As I read, I began looking at my own heart. I began to see my own critical spirit, my rigid perspective and my judgmental attitudes. It took a lot for God to get my attention so that spiritual maturity could start happening inside my soul. For the first time in my life, I saw a gap between the attitude Jesus had toward the church and the attitude I had. The gap was so massive! I was so far from what the Bible taught a right attitude toward God's church should be.

That is where my real repentance and brokenness before God began. When I gave Him permission, Jesus began putting His finger on every attitude I held that He wanted changed in my relationship to the church.

When I began to look at the church through His eyes rather than just my own, my heart began a gigantic adjustment. What do you think Jesus saw when He was on the cross? What was He thinking when He hung there suspended between two worlds in agony with His life's blood oozing out of His veins? We only know a few words Jesus spoke before He died. But the Bible makes clear when Jesus died on the cross, He "gave Himself up," not just for individuals but for the church.

> For the first time, I saw the gap between the attitude Jesus had toward the church and the attitude I had. The gap was massive!

He had a vision of imperfect people like you and me all over the world, gathered into divine groups! Meeting every week! Being corrected and obedient to His Word! Locking arms with each other in ministry and witness to the world! What a divine strategy! What an incredible design! What a marvelous creation of God! When I really saw it for the first time, I knew it was worth it to give the rest of my life for the church.

Eleven Biblical and Practical Reasons for Connection

As I have studied both the scriptures and church history, I have come to some conclusions about the imperfect visible church, denominational families and the way God is working through all of these various "tribes." Because so much is at stake in our collective mission, I am a staunch advocate for congregations maintaining strong denominational and fellowship connections. Let me offer eleven biblical and practical reasons why I have come to this conclusion.

1. The Bible teaches Christians to be *interdependent*, not independent. Paul describes the church as "the whole body, joined and held together by every supporting ligament, growing and building itself up in love" (Eph 4:16). We never see in the scripture a case for separation. The climate for healthy witness to the world is always the prayer of Jesus, "that all of them may be one, Father" (John 17:21). In his impulsiveness, Paul had such a sharp disagreement with Barnabas that he parted company with him (Acts 15:39). In later and more mature years, Paul admitted it was his mistake (2 Tim 4:11). I have watched enough people in ministry over the years to learn that impulsive decisions to separate ourselves when we are younger are usually regretted when we are older. We will talk about the few historical exceptions to this later.

> I have watched enough people in ministry over the years to learn that impulsive decisions to separate when we are younger are usually regretted when we are older.

The concept above is widely accepted and understood in the secular world. Jesus taught that "the people of this world are more shrewd in dealing with their own kind than are the people of the light" (Luke 16:8). Business leaders flock to Steven Covey seminars and pay thousands of dollars to listen to him teach "interdependence is a higher value than independence."[2] This principle has its foundation in scripture and it should be lived out within the church.

2. Many non-denominational fellowships act like denominational families. During these past five years NCS has worked with eighteen different denominational groups. We have also worked with church leaders from several non-denominational fellowships. It is our experience that non-denominational groups publish materials, have conferences together, find ways to help churches during pastoral transition, offer help when a local church is in crisis or has a moral failure, hold training events and conferences for ministers and lay leaders, provide schools for their young people and find ways to send and support missionaries. These non-denominational fellowships certainly operate with a different form of church government compared to denominationally-connected churches, but in many ways they act just like denominational families! They do so because they have learned across the years that

> In the Old Testament, there were no independent Jews; everyone had a tribe.

achieving the mission of Christ requires Christians to lock arms and work together.

3. In the Old Testament, there were no independent Jews; everyone had a tribe. The Bible teaches that the church is the new Israel of God (Gal 6:16) and the fulfillment of the covenant God made with Abraham (Gen 12:2-3; Gal 3:8, 14-16). In many ways, denominational families and fellowships can be likened to the Old Testament "tribes" of Israel. As you study the journey of God's people, God had everyone connected, there were no independent Jews! At times they did not get along with each other, and they certainly had their share of challenges, but they were all Israelites. They were all identified as the people of God, and every one of them was connected to a tribal family.

4. Denominations are in many ways like large spiritual families. If you have ever been in a denominational or fellowship family, have you noticed how many people know other people from across the country? People seem to all be related to each other. The wider body of Christ through a denomination or fellowship offers Christians "family relationships" with other believers that extends far beyond the local church.

5. In a few instances in church history, people have felt compelled to make decisions that caused them to separate from the visible church. The protestant reformers like Martin Luther (Lutherans) and John Knox (Presbyterians) are examples. John Wesley, the father of Methodism, was a loyal member of the Church of England until his death. The Evangelical Awakening God created through his life led to the founding of the Methodist church as a denomination after he died. As I have observed, however, there is a huge difference between these men and someone who leaves a denomination or fellowship family today. Most separations today are not over burning spiritual issues but over polity, personality conflicts or spiritual immaturity.

God gives us a clear word that is not very popular these days in the North American church: "Obey your leaders and submit to them, for they are keeping watch over your souls and will give an account. Let them do this with joy and not with sighing—for that would be harmful to you (Heb 13:17, NRSV). Jesus teaches that there is a direct relationship between submission to authority and great faith (Matt 8:5-10). I challenge you to be loyal to your judicatory, denominational family or fellowship. It is the right thing to do. Submit to those God has placed in authority over you. Do your best to make their work "a real joy" because of their contact with you. Make your attitude about the church positively contagious! If you do, God's promise is that you will find this to be of great "personal advantage" (Heb 13:17).

> Most separations today are not over burning spiritual issues but over polity, personality conflicts, or spiritual immaturity.

6. The genius of connectedness to a denomination or fellowship is that it provides local churches the opportunity to do together what no church can do separately. Thousands of Southern Baptist Convention (SBC) churches have been started, missionaries have been sent, and Christian leaders have been educated and trained because of the Cooperative Program. The church polity of the SBC is built on a foundation of local church autonomy and every church is congregational and independent, creating its own set of unique governmental challenges. Although there are some great Baptist churches God has raised up, the SBC Directors of Mission who have attended NCU all affirm there is no greatness as a spiritual movement without agenda harmony. Local churches must cooperate

> Make your attitude toward the church positively contagious! God's promise is that you will find this to be of great personal advantage.

with other local churches for the kingdom to multiply with great effectiveness.

The genius behind the thousands of Methodist churches that have multiplied is the cooperation of Methodism in apportionments and active connection to districts and conferences. Methodist churches working together do what no local church could ever do alone. My friend, Dr. Barry Carpenter, Director of New Church

& Congregational Development for the 900 churches in the Kentucky Conference, affirms that the secret of the Methodist movement historically has been its ability to gain agenda harmony for the health and multiplication of the church.

NCS has its direct roots in both the Nazarene and Wesleyan denominations. Dr. Tom Nees oversees evangelism and church growth for the Church of the Nazarene, Rev. Phil Stevenson oversees resourcing for The Wesleyan Church in a similar way—together they service 6,700 congregations in the U.S. and Canada. Both Tom Nees and Phil Stevenson affirm the principle that the key to denominational growth in the past has been the denominational ability to gain agenda harmony for the health and multiplication of local churches. When local churches come together and lock arms, they are able to do what no church can do separately. NCS has begun working with some synods in the Evangelical Lutheran Church of America. We are finding the same principles apply with the ELCA that also apply to the SBC, United Methodist, Nazarene, Wesleyan, Evangelical Friends, Independent Christian Churches and others. The structure may be different, but wherever the church is healthy, it is the result of churches gaining agenda harmony and doing together what no local church can do alone.

> People from different denominational families can walk hand in hand without seeing eye to eye.

7. People from different denominational families can walk hand in hand without seeing eye to eye. A key person on our NCS Team is Phil Spry, founder of TellStart. We come from very different theological backgrounds, but under the NCS umbrella we work together helping launch healthy churches in numbers of different denominational families.

When I think of my friendship with Phil, I am reminded of the Old Testament story of Jehu and Johonadab, two very different leaders. "...Jehu greeted him and said, 'are you in accord with me, as I am with you?' 'I am,' Johonadab answered. 'If so,' said Jehu, 'give me your hand.' So he did..." (2 Kings 10:15).

To be "in accord" means we extend our hand of fellowship to everyone following the Savior. They may not be part of our denomination, but our Lord taught clearly, "whoever is not against you is for you" (Luke 9:50). I had a pastor write to me when he found out I was working with people beyond my theological tradition. He was concerned and thought we should consider only working with Wesleyan groups. Here in part, was the reply I sent to him.

> Judicatories must refocus their activities, rekindle their spirit and keep taking risks just like their forefathers did!

"Many of our current NCS Partners are within the Wesleyan tradition. But the NCS Board of Directors has determined that in the spirit of John Wesley, we should serve wherever God gives us opportunities. John Wesley said to George Whitfield when they were at theological odds, "Is your heart one with my heart? Then give me your hand" (2 Kings 10:15-16). As the Lord opens doors for NCS to work—wherever judicatories desire renewal, ReFocusing, church planting and Parent training—if their hearts are right, we will join hands with them. We believe we can walk hand in hand with numbers of different denominational groups without seeing eye to eye on every issue. Billy Graham has set us a tremendous example in this way and we hope to follow his spirit and attitude."

8. Denominational families remain strong when they find ways to regularly review how God has worked in their history. The people of Israel had a way of reviewing their corporate memory and the activity of God among them. One example was the Israelite crossing of the Jordan River as they entered the Promised Land. Joshua commanded each tribe to set up a stone to remember how God had worked a miracle in the crossing (Josh 4:4-9).

John Dawson writes, "It is a dangerous thing to lose the knowledge of the past. One of the greatest needs of the church is a sense of her history and destiny."[3] After the people of God entered the Promised Land, established their land, properties and families, a very tragic thing occurred. It is the same thing that occurs to every denominational family that establishes itself but does not find ways to self-renew. What happens is that the next generation does not experience "the spirit" and sacrifice that shaped the denomination's founding. The people of the denomination no longer grow up in tents; they grow up in buildings. They do not experience a large amount of laboring and sacrificing. They only experience enjoying the labor and sacrifice of a previous generation.

The solution to this organizational and spiritual phenomenon is for judicatories to regularly review God's activity. They must renew their structures, refocus their activities, rekindle their spirit and keep taking risks just like their forefathers did. The Israelites did not experience this renewal and so after the first generation died, "another generation grew up, who knew neither the Lord nor what He had done for Israel" (Jud 2:10).

Israel's experience is a warning to the church, the new Israel of God. All these things in Israelite history "occurred as examples, to keep us from setting our hearts" on the wrong things (1 Cor 10:6). As a lay leader, pastor or judicatory leader, remember to review the activity of God. The lesson is clear—never forget the days of the tents!

9. Sectarian attitudes that have caused denominational families to be highly critical of one another are slowly being cleansed out of the church. All denominational families have great strengths and face similar problems. If you grew up in a typical denominational climate, chances are good you were taught that your denominational family was *very* right and all the other "tribes" in God's church were *very* wrong. You probably heard some say the chances were good that many people from the other tribes might not even make it to heaven. This sectarian attitude created great zeal to get people to join the "right tribe." The words of Paul are instructive, "I can testify about them that they are zealous for God, but their zeal is not based on knowledge" (Rom 10:2). Thank God much of that sectarian, critical spirit is dying away among denominational families.

I am not advocating that we erase denominational distinctives, blur theological emphases or downplay church heritage. I have a number of good friends outside my Wesleyan theological heritage who disagree strongly with me on certain issues. The Scriptures are clear: "There is one body and one Spirit...one Lord, one faith, one baptism, one God and Father of all..." (Eph 4:4-6). There is and should be incredible diversity within the broader church of Jesus Christ.

> When denominational leaders from varied theological backgrounds gather at NCU and begin sharing, they realize they all face the same challenges, grapple with similar issues, and they like each other!

What we should contend for is unity of spirit, without expecting uniformity of practice or belief. It takes all kinds of churches to reach all kinds of people. People who attend the Denominational Leaders Training Track at New Church University come from a variety of theological backgrounds, but when they all get in a room and begin sharing, they realize they all face the same challenges, grapple with similar issues, and they like each other!

10. Jesus is present in very imperfect local churches, judicatories and denominational families. In the Book of Revelation, we see the resurrected and ascended Christ reappear to the apostle John on the island of Patmos more than fifty years after Pentecost. While the church had spread and grown, there were numbers of churches far from perfect. In detail, Jesus tells John what to write to them. Here you may find one or more things you can identify with regarding the church you attend.

The encouraging thing, despite their problems and challenges, Jesus still walks in the middle of the church! Many are working hard. "Some of them may be forsaking their first love" (Rev 2:4). Some people may be "afraid of suffering" and sacrifice (Rev 2:10). Some are morally not where they should be (Rev 2:21). Some are in a state of spiritual deadness and need to "wake up" (Rev 3:1-2). Some seem to be tired (Rev 3:8) or are spiritually lukewarm (Rev 3:15-16).

> Denominations provide a great history, multiple benefits and enormous spiritual opportunities to their members.

With all these problems, what an incredible comfort to know Jesus is still among us. Be encouraged! He is here and walking in the middle of your church!

11. Denominations and fellowships provide a great

history, multiple benefits and enormous spiritual opportunities to their members. My father is a highly committed Christian and loyal member of a denominational family. He is not a pastor. Before retirement, he was a very successful executive manager in a large corporation. I will never forget a conversation we had back in 1989, when I was grappling with what I perceived to be the imperfections of our denominational family. I can still hear him talking to me in love as he detailed a list of all the benefits and opportunities our family unit had and was receiving because we were an active part of a denominational family.

> Denominations are not just the work of men. Though imperfect, they have been raised up to do the work of God, they are holy and should be treated with respect.

Twenty Benefits of Denominations & Fellowship Families

Denominations are not just the work of men. Even though imperfect, they have been raised up to do the work of God; they are holy and should be treated with reverence and respect. What follows are some things about spiritual legacy that I can still hear my father teaching me. Because I am in full-time ministry, I have added some of my own learning from across the years.

1. It was the church that came to our community and led your grandparents to Christ.

2. It was the church that created the opportunity for your mother and me to meet when we were teenagers.

3. It was the church that led both of us to Christ and nurtured our faith.

4. It was in the church that we were married and committed our home to God.

5. It was into the church that you were born and given back to God when you were young.

6. It was the church that provided and created the climate that led you to Christ.

7. It was the church that provided religious instruction and training for you during your childhood.

8. It was the church that provided youth activities and opportunities for you during adolescence to stay spiritually connected while facing temptation and secular pressures.

9. It was the church that sponsored and provided a Christian college for you to attend.

10. It was the church that, through its college connection, provided you with the Christian life companion you have.

11. It was the church that created the atmosphere that ultimately led to your call from God into full-time Christian ministry.

12. It was the church that, in your beginning days, gave you opportunities to exercise your call to preach.

13. It was the church that provided you with theological education.

14. It was the church that provided spiritual accountability, licensed and ultimately ordained you into the Christian ministry.

15. It was the church that assessed you as a church planter and gave you a place to serve.

16. It is the church that continues to provide you with the moral and spiritually accountability the Bible teaches every minister must have.

17. It is the church that, through your schooling and places of service, provides you a rich set of life-long relationships with friends and colleagues in ministry.

18. It is the church that allows you to freely participate in her government and voice your concerns at the appropriate time.

19. It is the church that continues to change and adjust her ministry to meet the needs of the world, and if you are patient, you will see God changing her as He has continued to do so for the past 2000 years.

20. When you leave or retire from the places you have served, it will be the church that provides continuity in your ministry transitions, so that your lifetime of work will not be lost but conserved.

After my father finished and I had reflected and prayed, I knew very clearly what God wanted me to do in my relationship with my denominational family.

You Can Build a Delightful Inheritance

Most of us are the children and grandchildren of some great people of faith. Whatever your denominational or fellowship roots, you have great men and women of faith in your tradition. We cannot divorce ourselves from our roots or heritage. It is important for us to biblically understand that the lives of the people preceding us were not just lived on earth. They are a great cloud of witnesses praying for and encouraging us even today! (Heb 12:1)

As I reflect on this truth, let me share how it became personal for me. It requires me to take you back to Kurtz, Indiana. I have stood on the hill where my grandfather is buried outside of Kurtz. His grave happens to be less than 500 yards from where the accident occurred that caused his death in 1953. The cemetery is on top of the hill, adjacent to the farm where he lived and worked. From that hilltop you can look down over the whole valley. You can see the white-frame church and the steeple rising

> When you leave or retire from the places you have served, it will be the church that provides continuity in ministry transitions, so that your lifetime of work will not be lost but conserved.

above the houses as the town's tallest building. It is a beautiful country sight.

I never met my grandfather, but I vividly remember standing by his grave and thinking about the spiritual legacy he left me. As I looked across the valley and saw the church from that hill, I could almost sense him standing beside me, with his hand on my shoulder, looking out across the valley as well. As a lay leader, he had spent literally thousands of hours traveling across that valley inviting people to church and to a relationship with Christ.

"The boundary lines have fallen for me in pleasant places, surely I have a delightful inheritance" (Psalm 16:6).

If he could have spoken to me from heaven, I know exactly what he would have said. "Larry, this is what I gave my life for. I gave my life for the church. In doing this, I was following the example of Jesus. Love God with all your heart. Be faithful with all your soul. Stay close to God's Word and let it continue to correct you. Most importantly, love the church!"

You may be reading this and thinking, "I do not have that kind of spiritual heritage." My word to you is, today you can begin building one for yourself, your family and all the generations that follow you. The testimony of David is my testimony and it can become yours as well: "The boundary lines have fallen for me in pleasant places, surely I have a delightful inheritance" (Psa 16:6).

Part Two

Lessons We Are Learning

6
Spiritual Strategic Planning

"We should make plans, counting on God to direct us."
Proverbs 16:9, LB

As a judicatory leader, pastor or lay leader, one of your primary church roles is to create a climate where "spiritual learning" can flourish. No Christian, local church or judicatory has "arrived." None of us knows everything we need to know to be all that God wants us to be. This is why we must always keep teachable and keep on learning. Churches and judicatories that thrive are those that never stop learning.

Becoming a Spiritual Learning Organization

In his book, *The Fifth Discipline*, Peter Senge accurately contends that not only individuals, but the organizations that will survive and thrive in the 21st century will be organizations committed to continual learning, growth and change. Every time we do a NewStart, ReStart, ReFocusing or Parent church project, we must learn what works and what does not work. What we learn we must *capture*, *catalogue* and *communicate*. We must never give up improving what we do. Every local church and judicatory must become a "learning laboratory" for us.

This learning requires us to keep perfecting the *feedback, listening loop* that fuels our learning. Proverbs 1:5 states, "let the wise listen and add to their learning, and let the discerning get guidance." How hungry are you to not stay where you are?

As a church leader, how committed are you to really listening to the people to whom you minister? Ask them sometime whether or not they perceive you to be a good listener. If you are a judicatory or denominational leader, how eager are you to seek feedback from those you serve? If you want to be both wise and effective, you must make a commitment to keep on learning.

> Churches and judicatories that thrive are those that never stop learning. What we learn we must *capture, catalogue* and *communicate*.

Learning is fueled by asking good questions. We are only told about one incident in the boyhood days of Jesus. He had been taken up to the temple when He was twelve and accidentally left behind by His parents.

The Scripture records, "After three days they found Him in the temple courts, sitting among the teachers, *listening to them* and *asking them questions*." All Jesus did was listen and ask questions. What was the result?

"Everyone who heard Him was amazed at His understanding and His answers" (Luke 2:46-47).

If we learn to ask the right question, we will always get the right answer. Beware of people who seem to imply they have all the answers. There are no simple formulas in building healthy churches and launching church multiplication movements. Every setting is different and requires contextualizing our learning, which requires learning to ask the right questions.

Beginning with God, Not Ourselves

Many churches today ask the wrong question when they begin their strategic thinking and planning. Churches that operate by asking, "What do *you* think we should do?" end up in a different place than churches that ask, "What does *God* think we should do?" We believe that to receive spiritual results, we must learn to think and always operate in a spiritual rather than just a "natural" or human way.

> Churches that operate by asking, "What do *you* think we should do?" end up in a different place than churches that ask, "What does *God* think we should do?"

We believe that building a spiritual learning organization and spiritual strategic planning go hand in hand. These require church leadership teams to begin with the right attitude. Churches with this attitude have learned that Christ is the head of the church, not any person or group. Together they seek to be "led by the Spirit" (Rom 8:14) and collectively "taught by the Spirit" (1 Cor 2:13; John 14:26). This attitude guides their decisions because Jesus "is the head of the body, the church; He is the beginning...so that in everything He might have the supremacy" (Col 1:18).

> The Bible is filled with repeated instructions on the importance of planning.

Paul teaches, "I pray that the eyes of your heart may be enlightened" (Eph 1:18). You may be thinking, "I have eyes in my heart?" Yes, we have not only physical eyes in our head, but spiritual eyes in our heart. We need our spiritual eyes alert to see what God wants us to see and decide the direction God wants us to go. As God's leader, you may be tempted to give up or feel confused. When this happens, ask God to give you spiritual sight. Ask Him to keep developing spiritual eyes within you. Just like Moses, when we have the right kind of eyes, "we persevere because we see Him who is invisible" (Heb 11:27). Spiritual sight develops perseverance as we plan and follow God's leading. There is a huge difference between a church that makes decisions based on what its leaders think *they* can do and a church that makes decisions based on what they believe *God* can do.

What practical steps can be taken to help a

church move its thinking from a human or natural level to a spiritual level? We have discovered that NewStart, ReStart, ReFocusing, Parent churches and judicatories make real progress when they understand what the Bible teaches about the planning process.

God Plans and Wants Us to Plan

We believe God is not against planning. God is a planning God! You have probably heard the saying, "If we fail to plan, we are planning to fail." Most people know this is true. The book of Proverbs is filled with repeated instructions on the importance of planning (i.e. Pro 12:5; 14:22; 15:22; 16:1, 3, 9; 19:21; 20:18; 21:5, 30). The Bible makes very clear, "We should make plans, counting on God to direct us" (Pro 16:9, LB). In Habakkuk 2, the Lord is communicating His plans to the prophet and instructs him, "Write the revelation [vision] down and make it plain on tablets so that those who read it may run with it...if it lingers, wait for it. It will come...but the righteous will live by faith" (Hab 2:2-4). From this passage, we are given some basic lessons about what we call "spiritual strategic planning."

- You must write your vision down.
- You must make it plain to read.
- If you make it plain to read, people can run with it.
- In vision and planning, timing is everything.
- You must wait for your vision to emerge.

David spiritually sought God in the strategic

planning process that surrounded the building of God's temple, and he received a plan from God. A key question every church leader must answer is, "Is God able to give us this same wisdom and ability to develop a clear plan to follow in what He is calling us to do for Him?" We believe the answer to that question is a resounding yes! *God is more anxious to reveal His plan to us than we are to seek it*! He has had specific plans for His people to fulfill from the beginning of time. "'I know the plans I have for you,' declares the Lord, 'plans to give you hope and a future'" (Jer 29:11).

When David began thinking about building the temple for the Lord, he was not haphazard. He knew he had to develop a plan. As he studied, wrote and ultimately completed the plan, he declared with joy and confidence, "All this (the plan for the temple), I have in writing from the hand of the Lord upon me. He gave me understanding in all the details of the plan" (1 Chr 28:19). David did not write the plan on his own, with his own wisdom or his own ideas. "The hand of the Lord was on him" (1 Chr 28:19). This is the key difference between *secular* strategic planning and *spiritual* strategic planning. David deeply sensed it was *God Himself* who had given him understanding in all of the step-by-step details that were required to build God's temple.

As a NewStart, ReStart, ReFocusing, Parent church or judicatory leader, you must believe today that God can give *you* and your team understanding! "Do not trust in your own understanding but...acknowledge Him and He will direct" (Pro 3:5-6) the development of the details. When you are led by God, planning your work and working your plan take on a deeply spiritual dimension.

In the New Testament, we see spiritual strategic planning taught and lived out in the life of Jesus. In His teaching, Jesus clearly assumes that thinking ahead is vital for the success of any building project (Luke 14:28-30). He teaches that planning is vital to any success or victory (Luke 14:31-33). It is interesting in this passage that Jesus clearly links planning with commitment and discipleship. In the past, many Christians have incorrectly felt that when a local church or judicatory engaged in strategic planning, they were moving from spiritual to non-spiritual work. Nothing could be further from the truth!

> When a group of people collectively seek to answer the question, "What does God think we should do?" this becomes a very spiritual process.

Eight Key Planning Questions

When a group of people collectively seek to answer the question, "What does God think we should do?" it becomes a very spiritual process. This is why we call it *spiritual strategic planning*.

Dr. Steve Andersen, a dedicated Christian layman who teaches in the School of Business & Technology at

Black Hills State University, is the one who taught me the following planning process. At New Church Specialties, we have now used it with scores of churches in church board renewal weekends and leadership team retreats.[1] The process is built on the principle of learning to ask the right questions.

There are eight spiritual strategic planning questions we use as we seek to answer the most important question, "What does God think we should do?" The eight questions are:

1. Who are we?   **MISSION & PURPOSE**

2. Where are we?   **NEEDS**

3. Where does God want us to go? **PRIORITIES & GOALS**

4. How are we going to get there? **PLANNING**

5. When will it be done?   **SCHEDULING**

6. Who is responsible for what? **DELEGATING**

7. How much will it cost?   **BUDGETING**

8. Did we do it?   **EVALUATING**

When we do spiritual strategic planning with a local church or judicatory, we walk through answering these questions with the team responsible for seeing the vision of the church realized. Great spiritual focus is created when a group of people come together and build a clear plan that addresses these issues as they seek to know what God wants them to do.

Agenda Harmony with God
for the Church

This leads us to ask this theological question. As we do spiritual strategic planning, is it possible for a group of Christians to really know what God is thinking? The apostle Paul answers this question in 1 Corinthians with an emphatic yes! He begins the discussion by emphasizing that every Christian ministry should not be built on "wise and persuasive words, but with a demonstration of the Spirit's power, so that people's faith will not rest on human wisdom, but on God's power" (1 Cor 2:4-5).

> Is it possible for a group of Christians to really know what God is thinking? The apostle Paul answers this question with an emphatic yes!

Paul then helps us understand how to help a church move into spiritual thinking when he writes, "No eye has seen, no ear has heard, no mind has conceived what God has prepared for those who love Him"—but God has revealed it to us by His Spirit" (1 Cor 2:9-10). I grew up thinking this passage was a reference to heaven, until I read the context. What Paul is teaching here is that there are issues we all need to understand beyond the *natural* realm, into the *spiritual* realm. What our eyes cannot see physically, what our ears cannot hear or our mind cannot conceive physically, God wants to reveal to us *spiritually*. Paul calls these the "deep things of God" (1 Cor 2:10).

He then says "who knows the thoughts of a person except the person's spirit within them?" (1 Cor 2:11). In other words, no one knows what I am thinking or what you are thinking except "our spirit" within us. "In the same way no one knows the thoughts of God except the Spirit of God" (1 Cor 2:11). The Holy Spirit knows what God is thinking. What an incredible truth and magnificent promise! Paul explains that as we lead God's church, "This is what we are to speak, not in words taught us by human wisdom but in words taught by the Spirit, expressing spiritual truths in spiritual words" (1 Cor 2:13).

The climate we operate in should be *spiritual* rather than natural or human. We should seek to move all of our strategic thinking into a spiritual rather than a natural realm. I wish I could say that everyone in the church will always be open to spiritual thinking, but sometimes they are not. Paul explains, "Those who are unspiritual do not receive the gifts of God's Spirit, for they are foolishness to them, and they are unable to understand them because they are spiritually discerned" (1 Cor 2:14, NRSV). Here is the million dollar question. In the strategic planning your church does, how much "spiritual discernment" is involved?

Paul describes the kind of people who should be leading God's church, as "those who are spiritual" (1 Cor 2:15, NRSV). He concludes the chapter with a great promise for every group of Christians in spiritual leadership when he says, "we have the mind of Christ" (1 Cor 2:16).

This passage of scripture leads us to some basic principles we should follow as we do spiritual strategic planning.

- Our greatest need is not to know what *we* are thinking, but what *God* is thinking.
- As Christian leaders, we have the Holy Spirit.
- The Holy Spirit knows God's thoughts.
- We can know what God is thinking.
- It is possible for us to have the mind of Christ.

The purpose of spiritual strategic planning is not to get everyone in the church to agree with "our agenda" but for us to collectively seek God's agenda. We want the mind of Christ. We want to answer questions such as, "Where does God want our church to go? What does God want us to do? What does God want us to attempt?" This is spiritual strategic thinking.

> The purpose of spiritual strategic planning is not to get everyone in the church to agree with "our agenda" but for us to collectively seek God's agenda.

This again leads us back to the premise of this book. When God's church enjoys unity and agenda harmony, she is unstoppable. Agenda harmony occurs when the church is working together for a common objective, with a common purpose, in a common spirit. As Paul describes it, 1) they are like-minded, 2) they have the same love, 3) they are one in spirit and 4) they are one in purpose (Phil 2:2).

When a local church or judicatory has a vision that people believe has come from the church's leadership team, it will sputter and most likely stall. But if people believe the vision being followed has truly come from God, the vision has a very high probability of being achieved. Do you remember the words of instruction from Gamaliel to the Sanhedrin regarding the early disciples? "For if their purpose or activity is of human origin, it will fail. But if it is from God, you will not be able to stop these men; you will only find yourselves fighting against God" (Acts 5:38-39). Clear spiritual vision that people deeply believe has come from God is unstoppable!

7

Begin with the End in Mind

"Suppose one of you wants to build a tower. Will he not first sit down and estimate the cost to see if he has enough money to complete it? For if he lays the foundation and is not able to finish it, everyone who sees it will ridicule him, saying, 'This fellow began to build and was not able to finish.'"
Luke 14:28-30

In his book, *The Seven Habits of Highly Effective People*, author Stephen Covey says that one habit all effective people have developed is the habit of "beginning with the end in mind."[1]

If you want to accomplish something significant, you must envision the end objective and then work backward. This idea, however, did not originate with Stephen Covey; it began with God.

Reflect on God's creation for a moment. In our world, everything is created twice. There is first the mental creation and then physical creation follows.

Planning Began In Creation

Everything you see around you in God's creation first began as a thought in God's mind. God had to think it before He created it. "God calls things that are not as though they were" (Rom 4:17). "The earth was formless and empty...and God said, 'Let there be light'" (Gen 1:2-3), "let the land produce vegetation, seed-bearing plants and trees" (Gen 1:11), "let the water team with living creatures...let the birds fly above the earth" (Gen 1:20). Everything God created had to be created twice. First God had to think it, He had to detail it in His mind, and then He had to create it physically.

The supreme expression of God's creation was the human family. "Let us make humankind in our image, according to our likeness" (Gen 1:26, NRSV). When God made us in His image, He gave us a capacity that He did not give any other of His creation. It is the capacity to create with our minds. The ability to plan actually flows out of our being created in the image of God.

Building A Church Action Plan

If you talk to a construction specialist, he or she will tell you that in the construction of a quality church building, every detail must be created on paper, before you start hammering the nails into place. The architect works with the client's ideas until a clear image of what is to be built comes into view. Then that image is put into a blueprint, an artist's conception, a virtual tour, and ultimately construction plans are developed.

All of this thinking and planning is regularly done by thousands of congregations every year before a single spade of dirt is turned for a new or remodeled church building. If you do not go through the discipline of thinking all of these details through before you begin, you may be in big trouble. If you decide that you do not want a wall here or a bathroom there, the cost goes up significantly to make those changes. There is an enormous price tag people pay when they build without thinking through the details.

> In our world, everything is created twice. There is first mental creation and then physical creation follows.

The same principles that apply in building a quality church building also apply in building a healthy church body. Whether your goal is to achieve the launch of a NewStart, ReStart, ReFocusing or Parent church, the future end objective of the project is where you begin. Then you work backward, asking yourself, "What is involved and necessary to achieve this?" You identify the issues, the components, and then you create a clear plan that includes them.

From our research, this essential habit of planning the future of the church is what most congregations do very poorly. We designed New Church University to help solve this problem. Before they attended NCU, over 90% of the churches with which we have worked operated with no written strategy or plan. A vast majority of churches feel the need to have a plan. What they lack is both opportunity and the training to develop their planning skills.

The unique feature of New Church University is that in multiple training tracks that correspond to the end objective desired (NewStart, ReStart, ReFocusing, etc.) the planning process itself has already been thought through. Church leaders feel an incredible relief when they do not have to start with a blank sheet of paper. We have studied over 500 church action plans and have learned that there are key issues good church action plans must address.

To get the right answer, you must ask the right question. At NCS, we identified seven key questions—answering them is what the NCU development team grappled with as we created the curriculum for New Church University. The key questions we believe church leaders must answer are:

1. Why are you doing this?
2. Where do you feel called?
3. Who will you reach?
4. What kind of church will it be?
5. With whom will you work to achieve this?
6. How and when will all this happen?
7. How much will it cost?[2]

The end in mind that we sought to achieve was a training event that would assist pastors and lay leaders working together to create a high quality Church Action Plan that answered these questions.

New Church University Curriculum

What emerged in the NCU curriculum were fifteen major components that all effective NewStart, ReStart & ReFocusing church plans have in common.[3] We believe each of these components should be thought through in building a ministry "blueprint" plan that is unique for each church. The distinctive feature of the training is that while the components are the same, every plan is different because of the way it is contextualized by individual leaders and churches.

We call the curriculum "New Church Blueprints." Brief descriptions of its major components are summarized below.

1. Divine Call & Passion: In spiritual work, everything begins with the call of God and a biblical passion to obey. The Bible is filled with

> Before they attended New Church University, over 90% of the churches we have worked with operated with no written strategy or plan.

examples of this (John 20:21). We believe biblical passion can be both caught and taught. Our goal at NCU is to create a climate where God rekindles the passion of leaders so they clearly confirm and articulate their call. Their plan should include a summary of their formal or informal assessment results, a brief summary of their background and journey to this point, and a list of life verses God has used to speak to them, confirming His direction for their ministry.

2. Intercession Strategy: We encourage every NewStart, ReStart, ReFocusing or Parent church leader to build an Intercession Team. We believe so strongly in this that we do not encourage a judicatory or denomination to approve a church plant or refocusing project unless the pastor has mobilized and is communicating regularly with at least 15 people who are covering the project in prayer. Their blueprint should include practical steps of how they plan to keep prayer and dependence on God central in all they do.

3. Ministry Focus Group: We encourage church leaders to clearly define the specific group of people they are called to reach and how they plan to connect with this group. We encourage them to survey and listen to at least 250 unchurched people who live in their target area. We encourage their plan to include a solid study of demographics. We provide worksheets that help them define their ministry focus group geographically, demographically, culturally, spiritually and numerically.[4]

4. Core Values: We provide teaching and practical exercises that help church leaders develop core values which form the foundation for their church's decision-making in the future. Core values help answer the question of why we do what we do. We assist church leaders in connecting the eight characteristics of a healthy church to their core values.

5. Vision Description: This section in blueprints helps answer the question, "What kind of church will it be?" We emphasize the difference between individual vision and shared vision that is owned by a group of people. We encourage the church leader to visualize the church three to five years in the future and write a description of it. We believe vision is like a Polaroid camera. It will be fuzzy at first, but if you give it to God and do not give up on it, it will become clearer over time as you move toward it.

6. Mission Statement: From the core values and description of the church, we encourage the church leader to develop a concise, popularized statement. My good friend, Aubrey Malphurs, teaches that it should be easy to memorize and small enough to put on a T-shirt.

7. Launch or ReFocusing Team Roles: In several components at NCU, the NewStart & ReStart training track is separated from the ReFocusing track. While both need a leadership team brought together, the process in which this is done is very different. The NewStart & ReStart tracks emphasize how to recruit launch team members and the various positions needed based on the anticipated size of the grand opening crowd. The ReFocusing track covers how to select team members, what to cover in ReFocusing meetings, and implementation steps to take.

> To get the right answer, you must ask the right question.

8. Agenda Harmony: In the introduction, we talked about

the importance of every church leader building agenda harmony. This subject is dealt with in all of our NCU training tracks, and practical suggestions are given as to how agenda harmony can be gained.

9. Relationships: This component is where we teach and emphasize the main theme of this book. We talk about the relationship between judicatory and denominational leaders and the local church from a biblical and practical viewpoint. We emphasize that all church health and church multiplication movements require people to love the denominational family or fellowship God has placed them in and to have agenda harmony with other church leaders. Our goal is to create a climate where the Holy Spirit can bring healing and a renewed commitment to love the church as much as Jesus does.

10. Timeline & Critical Milestones: In this component, we teach church leaders to do what we call "low-cost project management." Staff and coaches assist NewStart, ReStart & ReFocusing leaders as they use post-it-notes to detail out the practical steps they need to take over the next eighteen to twenty-four months. We encourage them to display these in a prominent place at home where they can regularly see what they must do to stay on track. Charles Hobbs teaches "the theory of accessibility," which explains that if you want to induct someone into a new habit or skill, you must keep that habit or skill directly accessible to them. You have probably heard the popularized version of this theory: "out of sight, out of mind."

11. Ministry Flow Chart: In this component, we help church leaders identify the probable path individuals will follow as they take spiritual steps of obedience, moving from "pre-Christian" to becoming a global disciple. Our goal is to assist church leaders in learning better how to create a climate the Holy Spirit can use. Each church must build a personal "ministry flow" plan to fit their discipleship strategy. This includes people being baptized, becoming self-feeding Christians, joining a Sunday School class or small group, joining the church, becoming a worshiper, getting involved in the church, using their spiritual gifts in meaningful ministry, becoming a tither, engaging in personal witnessing and the list goes on. Rick Warren calls this the Life Development Process, uses a baseball diagram and ties it in with education and assimilation.[5] It is not important to us what a church calls it or even how it is implemented. We just know that every church must have "a process of making disciples," and the steps involved must be clearly thought through.

> Every church must have a process of making disciples and the steps involved must be clearly thought through.

12. Determining the Right Location: Ministry leaders must evaluate where the vision and plan God is giving them should be housed. Where can the new church met? Will the current location need to be remodeled to achieve the vision? Will the congregation have to relocate? Location is a critical issue church leaders must address.

13. Outreach & Advertising Strategy: In this component, we assist church leaders in planning both large and small attraction events, as well as designing the church's "image" in the community. Logo, letterhead, business cards, website, etc., are all part of this. The visitor-flow strategy the church builds must be detailed enough to achieve what we call "critical

> We teach that if the vision is simply for one church, the vision is both too small and unbiblical.

mass." We have a close working relationship with my good friend Phil Spry from TellStart and encourage churches to consider using TellStart because of the great results many churches have had with it.[6]

14. Church Multiplication Strategy: Even though most church leaders attend NCU to build a plan for one church, we teach that if the vision is simply for one church, the vision is both too small and unbiblical. The Bible calls us to multiply. We give practical steps churches can take to insure that healthy church multiplication is put into the DNA of every congregation with which we work. Before receiving NCU training, every person is required to sign an entrance agreement. This includes a commitment to help sponsor or parent a new church within three years of attending NCU.

15. Comprehensive Budget & Stewardship Develop-

ment: Every church must have a plan to fund its ministry. This includes discipling people to take the spiritual step of obedience and move from being "tippers" to becoming faithful "tithers." Especially for the NewStart & ReStart training track, it includes thinking through income, projected expenses and cash flow from the time the planter moves on-site to the time the church reaches financial self-support status.

The NCS logo was specifically designed to communicate our vision of New Church University training. The logo includes a triangle and measuring rule, tools architects use to create "blueprints." If you count the spaces on the measuring rule, there are fifteen spaces, corresponding to the fifteen components of a high quality, Church Action Plan. The world that  extends over "new church" represents the global nature of God's calling to us. The logo is also designed to represent an "umbrella," covering the multiple of specialties a church health and church multiplication movement needs.

The more we watch new and existing congregations develop church action plans, the more we are beginning to see natural links that exist between the components. For example, there is a very close relationship between component 3, Ministry Focus Group, and component

13, Outreach & Advertising Strategy. Once churches have a clear ministry focus group, they must develop a plan to "connect" with their community through outreach and attraction events. Every church's ministry and "connection" will be different, based on community location and needs.

> Spiritual strategic planning is a skill that can be learned.

Another natural link is between component 5, Vision Description, and component 7, the Launch or ReFocusing Team. Church leaders must communicate a clear vision to build a solid team. There is a direct relationship between the articulation of our vision and having effective recruiting conversations.

When people in ReFocusing churches ask why we do not simply do a church health evaluation and have the church work on its "minimum factor,"[7] our reply is that we do. However, we have worked with hundreds of churches now and have realized that churches need more than evaluation and two or three implementation strategies. They need to learn how to plan and to plan holistically. We believe that spiritual strategic planning is a skill that can be learned!

It is not the purpose of this book to explain everything we are learning through the delivery of New Church University. But we *are highly committed* to capturing and cataloguing our on-going learning so that every New Church University event is improved.

8

Needed:
Not Just a Conference,
a Training System

*"If as one people they speak the same language...
nothing they plan to do will be impossible for them."*
Genesis 11:6

It is important for us to note that New Church Specialties is a *training system ministry*, not a conference-centered ministry. At most church training conferences today, great ideas are offered, people are inspired, notebooks are filled, resources are purchased, but when trainees leave the event, they do not have a plan to implement or the accountability required to ensure its execution.

We have learned that while New Church University is a very valuable training tool and important for creating a church health and multiplication climate, by itself it is insufficient to achieve the results judicatory and local church leaders need.

Church training must be combined with a well-thought out judicatory support and accountability system.

The NCU Training System

New Church University has been designed with the goal of building what we call "new church blueprints." Our objective is to assist NewStart, ReStart and ReFocusing church leaders to develop high quality church action plans they think through with their leadership team prior to implementation. With over 3,000 church leaders attending New Church University in the past 4 years, we have captured and catalogued some of the mistakes church leaders make in the process. Out of our learning, we have built what we call the NCU training system. Following are five steps we believe are critical in the training process and must not be violated.

> Church training must be combined with a well-thought out judicatory support and accountability system.

The first step involves a formal or informal assessment. NewStart and ReStart church planters cannot be fully enrolled at NCU unless they have passed this first step. A number of our denominational partners such as the Wesleyan Church and the Church of the Nazarene provide formal Assessment Centers for this purpose. Lonnie Bullock, NCS Senior Consultant, has been trained by Chuck Ridley in behavioral interviewing assessment and provides this service to our judicatory partners who request it.[1]

In unique situations, we allow judicatory leaders to send someone to NCU after an informal assessment has been done by them. This is usually done when the person's track record and past ministry effectiveness makes clear that he or she has a high degree of church planting capability. With few exceptions, our policy is that no potential planter is allowed to attend NCU without the approval of his or her judicatory leader. We also highly recommend that churches attending the NCU ReFocusing track have a church health evaluation done prior to arrival.

As a free benefit to all NCU enrollees, another service we provide is a Spiritual Gifts Mix Analysis (SGMA). This is sent to the enrollee when they register. It is designed to help enrollees identify their spiritual gift mix, as well as identify strengths and growth opportunities as they begin their NewStart, ReStart or ReFocusing project.

The second step in the system involves learning terminology. Every enrollee is asked to pass the NCU Entrance Exams. This requirement is not designed to intimidate anyone: we provide enrollees the terms, the definitions and the answer key. NewStart, ReStart, ReFocusing, Parenting, agenda harmony, intercession strategy, ministry focus group, ministry flow chart, comprehensive budget, stewardship development plan and 100 other terms we use have been clearly defined.

Our goal is simply to "ramp people up" by establishing a common language. We have found this improves the learning experience at NCU enormously. There is clear biblical support for this concept in the book of Genesis. God understood the power of a common language in building agenda harmony. At the tower of Babel He said,

"If as one people they speak the same language… nothing they plan to do will be impossible for them" (Gen 11:6). As a result, God confused their language so the people would be halted from doing more evil.

On the day of Pentecost, this confusion of language was restored through the Holy Spirit's miraculous work of proclaiming the gospel in multiple languages. The practical principle we are learning is clear. To launch and sustain church health and church multiplication movements, we must establish and use a common language. This is another critical step in the achievement of agenda harmony by judicatories and denominations.

> God understood and articulated the power of a common language in building agenda harmony.

The third step we use in the system involves the beginning of a first-draft Church Action Plan prior to arrival. We encourage people to register eight to twelve weeks before the training event. When people register, they receive an instructional CD that includes a large majority of the new church blueprints support material. They are asked to go through the material and are given two action plans as models to aid their thinking. Upon arrival, everyone is given an accountability sheet to determine how far along they are in the development of their plan. We create network groups at NCU based in part on their stage of action plan development.

The fourth step in the NCU Training System is the actual NCU training event itself. There is a planned balance of large group presentation (65%), network group feedback (20%) and individual time (15%). (Many highly motivated leadership teams work on their plan even during breaks and evenings.) The purpose of the network groups is to facilitate discussion, raise questions related to the particular component presented, and respond to questions that may arise from network group members as they continue to develop their action plan. We use NCS trained coaches to facilitate the network groups. When a judicatory contracts with us to deliver an entire NCU for them, level one coaches' training is normally done the day prior to the event.

The fifth step in the system is securing a nationally qualified coach. This is where many ReFocusing churches try to cut corners. We cannot overemphasize the importance of sticking to the system! We are finding that long-term change within a congregation requires the development of a plan, a first-class training event designed to perfect that plan and a qualified coach who assists the pastor and congregation in being held accountable for implementing the plan. While we strongly recommend, we do not currently require churches in the ReFocusing training track to secure a coach. We leave that decision to the pastor, the church leadership team or the judicatory leader.

Our policy with NewStart and ReStart church plants is much different regarding the securing of a qualified coach. We believe a judicatory is playing Russian roulette with the church plant if this is not a requirement. For this reason, we do not train church planters who will not commit to securing a coach. We have learned that too much is at stake for us to operate any other way. At NCS, we are so committed to the NCU training system that we provide a 100% satisfaction guarantee. If, at the end of using the training system, you do not feel NCU has met or exceeded your expectations, we will fully refund your tuition.

> We are so committed to the NCU training system that we provide a 100% satisfaction guarantee.

As New Church University has developed, we have continued to add more training tracks to meet the needs of our judicatory partners. The delivery of certain training tracks may vary at particular events, but we currently have the following tracks developed: 1) NewStart churches, 2) ReStart churches, 3) ReFocusing churches, 4) Parent churches, 5) Post-Launch Planters, 6) Denominational Supervisors (judicatory leaders), 7) Coaching Level 1 and 8) Coaching Level 2. NCU is currently held in various church locations across North America. As we continue to learn and grow, we are committed to providing the finest training system and coaching for NewStart, ReStart, ReFocusing and Parent church leaders available today.

9
Desire, Resources & Climate

"Then the Lord replied: 'Write down the revelation [vision] and make it plain on tablets so that a herald may run with it. For the revelation [vision] awaits an appointed time; it speaks of the end and will not prove false. Though it linger, wait for it; it will certainly come and will not delay...but the righteous will live by faith.'"
(Habakkuk 2:2-4)

I am grateful to NCS Senior Consultants Phil Stevenson and Lonnie Bullock for the development of what we now call "the 3 circles." This has been very instrumental in helping numbers of local church and judicatory leaders. We have discovered that Desire, Resources and Climate are all critical in launching and sustaining effective church health and church multiplication movements. Let me explain the chart on page 133 that illustrates what we are learning.

Every church health and church multiplication movement within a judicatory begins with desire. This presupposes basic knowledge about the components of launching and sustaining a movement, and the development of vision and passion that motivates us to facilitate change. We are learning that desire begins with knowledge. God says, "My people are destroyed for lack of knowledge" (Hosea 4:6). Many judicatories would like to enjoy the benefits of a church health and church multiplication movement, but they do not understand how to get there from where they currently are. Their future is being destroyed simply because of what they do not know. This is why we believe that many times desire begins with knowledge. Judicatories must be educated in the basic components of what church health and church multiplication movements require.

> **The future of some judicatories is being destroyed simply because of what they do not know.**

Developing A Judicatory Vision

The development of a specific vision for a particular judicatory follows the exposure to basic knowledge. If God had His full way and a movement happened, what would look different? What would be different? How differently would people think and act? If God moved in a great way and did "immeasurably more than we could ask or imagine" (Eph 3:20), how would we know it happened? The vision for a church health and multiplication movement must begin in the hearts of the judicatory leaders. It does not end with them and it must become a "shared vision" through building agenda harmony. But the mental image and visual picture of the future being different than the present is the greatest gift a leader can give to those who follow.

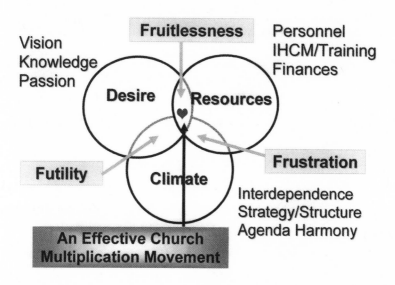

We are learning that this kind of judicatory vision does not come all at once. It will take time to develop. It is normally like a Polaroid photo; it will be fuzzy at first, but it will become clearer and clearer as time goes on, as it is adjusted and perfected. God reminds us, "Write it down... if it lingers, wait for it...it will come! (Hab 2:2-3) If the knowledge is present and the vision is becoming clearer, the components are in place for God to help the judicatory leaders begin gathering around themselves pastors and lay leaders who share the vision for a movement to begin.

Directly linked with knowledge and vision is

passion. There is no church health and church multiplication movement without a passion for it to be developed. There can and should be no doubt or question within your mind that, with God's power, you can achieve the spiritual desires God is placing in your heart. God would never have given you these specific Christ-centered desires for a healthy movement unless He knew you were capable of achieving them.

Every one of us has a God-given, built-in "governor." Paul teaches that our abilities and spiritual leadings modify our desires. "God is at work in you, to will and to do, according to His good purpose" (Phil 2:13). Centered in God's will, your desire for a church health and church multiplication movement can and should become a reality! To aid you in the development of desire and passion, the following are some practical steps you can take to bring God's vision for your judicatory into reality. Begin this process with prayer and waiting on God. Do not just talk to God about it; listen for God's voice. Record any ideas or impressions God gives you as you seek His wisdom. Be definite and exact concerning what you believe God wants your judicatory team to accomplish.

> Centered in God's will, your desire for a church health and church multiplication movement can and should become a reality.

Ask yourself the question, "If we go after this, what

part does God expect me to play in achieving this?" To succeed, there are some divine moments we will have to have from God. But there is also a part we must play in this process.

A key part of this is your commitment to creating a detailed plan for achieving the vision God is giving you. In very specific detail, write everything out. Dr. J.B. Chapman wrote years ago, "Thoughts disentangle themselves when they pass through the lips and the fingertips." As you detail the plan, remember it will not be static, but will continue to emerge and change. You cannot wait until the plan is perfect to begin. There is no perfect plan. Do not procrastinate or sit around waiting for God to begin His part. He is waiting to see if you are serious about your part.

After you begin, you must regularly review the plan God has given you. Keep perfecting it. Seek to be led by the Lord in His will. As His Spirit confirms His plans to you, see in your mind's eye and feel in your heart and believe with your will that your God-given desires have already begun to be fulfilled and that God Himself is big enough to do it! The One who calls you is faithful and He will do it (1 Thess 5:24).

Through the power of a God-given vision and the spiritual desire that God grants to those who long for it, God can and does give to people who seek it, that something within them that recognizes no such word as impossible and an inner power that accepts no such reality as failure!

Long-Term Judicatory Decision Making

It is an undeniable fact that the decisions made by a judicatory leader or members of a judicatory leadership team today will greatly affect the church tomorrow. In the Scriptures this is clearly seen in the life of Hezekiah. Hezekiah represents a leader who was only concerned about himself. He was in great need of refocusing. Hezekiah was selfish, shortsighted and proud. 2 Chronicles 32 tells us that after Hezekiah was healed of his sickness, envoys were sent by the rulers of Babylon to see his kingdom and ask how God had healed him. In reality, God was testing Hezekiah to see what was really in his heart (2 Chr 32:31), and Hezekiah failed the test.

> God can and does give to people who seek it, that something within them that recognizes no such word as impossible and an inner power that accepts no such reality as failure!

When the prophet Isaiah came to him and confronted him about his leadership failure to think long-term, Hezekiah's only response was that he was happy he would be taken care of "in peace and security" during his lifetime (2 Kings 20:19). This principle applies not only to Hezekiah and Old Testament Israel, but also to the church today. Lay leaders, pastors and judicatory leaders all make decisions, and the churches they serve reap the consequences of those decisions thirty, forty, fifty years later, many times after they are gone.

For example, a highly influential lay leader fights proposed changes that will reach new people and wins the battle. The church begins to decline because of the decision. Peace and security win over risk and opportunity. A denomination or judicatory decides it is not interested in starting new churches. The focus on planting churches declines. Thirty years later, even when new leaders are in place, the impact of that decision still has a profound effect on the growth and development of that denomination or judicatory.

Starting new churches is hard work. ReStarting churches is many times messy. ReFocusing churches is a process filled with potential conflict and possibly high degrees of criticism. Parenting requires the possible sacrifice of both members and money. As church leaders, it would be so much easier to simply want "peace and security in my lifetime." It would be much more convenient to say, "Let the leader that follows me handle these hassles." However, to make any of these decisions today is to decide on the decline of the church tomorrow.

> As a result of the decisions church leaders make today, the churches they serve reap the consequences of those decisions long after they are gone.

Our challenge to church leaders is to always make today's decisions based on what is best for the church we love in the next generation, not on what is best or easy for us. Dr. Bill Sullivan writes, "The best time to plant a new tree was 20 years ago. The next best time is today!"1 In our church, we do not just want peace and security; give us risk and opportunity! The development of this kind of desire is foundational to launching church health and church multiplication movements.

Raising Resources

The second "circle" we have discovered deals with resources. Once a judicatory develops a desire for a church health and church multiplication movement, it must deal with the issue of raising resources. We have learned resources include three things: personnel, the provision of quality training and finances. Personnel resources include the recruitment of NewStart, ReStart, ReFocusing and Parent church leaders. To launch a movement, we must build a team of pastors and lay leaders who believe in what God is calling our local churches and judicatories to be.

Once we have recruited the right people, we must provide high quality training for them. This will require specialized training for NewStart churches, ReStart churches, ReFocusing churches and Parent churches. It will require assisting these leaders to develop high quality church action plans. It will require coaching and mentoring that assists in holding them accountable for the implementation of their plans. It will require training in church health evaluation and assisting every leader to understand and implement church health strategies in the planning process.

Fueling any movement also requires raising money for ministry. There is a multitude of ways judicatories are doing this. To assist in this process, NCS trains NewStart and ReStart planters to seek

In our church, we do not just want peace and security...give us risk and opportunity!

multiple sources for their church plant funding. We have discovered there are multiple "pockets" for church plant giving. Below is a beginning list for church leaders to use in raising church plant resources.

1. Planter Bi-vocational Income. Many planters doing a "parachute plant" without strong parent churches need this because of the time it takes to gather a launch team. Many planters also find involvement in the workplace is a great way to connect with people in the community.

2. Planter Spouse Income. This is not required in every situation, but it has been a tremendous help in hundreds of church plant situations. Many spouses support the church plant directly by adding this income stream so the church can be launched effectively.

3. Family Wealth. Numbers of church planters have had equity in a home or family business that has been used to launch a new church.

4. Family and Friends One-Time Gift. We encourage planters to contact their "Christmas card list" of family and friends, asking for a one-time gift. This is normally used to help cover start-up expenses.

5. Family and Friends Monthly Support. Beyond the one-time gift, we encourage planters to seek out family and friends willing to provide monthly support for 12-24 months until the church has reached self-support status.

6. Parent Church Support. We define a parent church as one that assumes major financial support of the church plant. Every strong, healthy church multiplication movement requires parent churches.

7. Sponsor Churches' Support. We define a sponsor church as the coming together of two or more churches to support a church plant. Every strong, healthy church multiplication movement needs dozens of sponsor churches.

> Fueling any movement requires raising money for ministry.

8. Gifts In Kind. Parent or sponsor churches, businesses or individuals sometimes give new churches gifts in kind, such as office equipment, computers, office space, etc. (Make sure you do not give the new church your leftovers.)

9. New Church Baby Shower. We have found a great way for parent and sponsor churches to support a church plant is to have the planter provide a list of specific things the new church needs. People are then encouraged to give the new church a "baby shower" of the needed items.

10. Launch Team Tithe & Offerings. We encourage planters to open a bank account as soon as possible, secure proper registration, and begin soliciting funds from the launch team and other interested donors.

11. Local Church Deputation Offerings. Wherever possible, we encourage church planters to travel throughout a judicatory as "home missionaries," sharing their vision and building agenda harmony, not only for their particular plant, but for everyone's participation in their judicatory's church multiplication movement.

12. Missions Budget. Many congregations are beginning to add the planting of a new church to their annual missions budget and are learning that church planting is a great way to help fulfill our mission next door.

13. Sunday School Classes & Small Groups. In some larger churches, Sunday School classes or small groups are teaming up to help sponsor a new church or provide a specific item the new church needs.

14. Foundation Funds. Some metro areas have established a Christian Community Foundation from which new churches can solicit funds if they are providing a needed community service.

15. Judicatory or Denominational Grant. This is the last financial source we name because we believe judicatories or denominations do not plant healthy churches; only local parent and sponsor churches do. The role of the judicatory is to help create the climate for healthy church multiplication, and to partner with local churches to assist them in sponsoring, etc. Healthy church multiplication movements always have the judicatory in a supportive role to the local church fueling the movement.

> Every strong, healthy church multiplication movement requires parent churches.

In the next chapter, we will deal with the principles and processes we have learned in developing the climate for church health and church multiplication.

10

Principles & Processes in Developing Climate

"Repent, then, and turn to God, so that your sins may be wiped out, that times of refreshing may come from the Lord."
Acts 3:19

As we seek to effectively develop church health and church multiplication movements within judicatories, we are learning some basic principles and implementing processes that assist in developing the right climate. The most important responsibility a judicatory leader has is the creation, development and nurture of *a climate* that is conducive to healthy, church multiplication. We will talk often in this chapter about climate, so let me define what we mean.

Climate: the prevailing attitude toward church health and church multiplication held by a critical mass of lay and pastoral leaders.

Many local church and judicatory leaders have a deep desire for the climate within their judicatory to change but what they need is an understanding of both the principles and processes involved in achieving this. Our history has taught us that programs, by themselves, are usually insufficient in transforming judicatory climate. At NCS, we have learned that the transformation of judicatory climate requires an attitude of interdependence (solid ecclesiology), clear strategy and structure and gaining agenda harmony. Below is a summary of some of the principles learned as we have helped judicatories develop church health and church multiplication climates.

Principles We Have Learned

We must *teach a correct doctrine of ecclesiology.* All of our NewStart, ReStart, ReFocusing & Parent Church training must begin with what we believe about the church. A change in behavior always flows out of a change in beliefs. The way the Holy Spirit changes people's beliefs is with correct teaching from the Word of God (Matt 22:29; Eph 3:10; 1 Tim 4:16; 2 Tim 3:16).

We must teach *a healthy local church is God's plan to transform the world.* Nothing has more life-changing, life-transforming power than a healthy local church. It is Jesus' plan to transform the world and usher in His kingdom. When the church is healthy, individual lives are transformed as people take spiritual steps of obedience in moving from pre-Christian to becoming global disciples (Matt 28:19-20).

We must *teach people to love the church.* Having a passion for the church is at the center of the heart of God. It also links us to the heart of people who lead the church. Christ "gave Himself up" for an imperfect church because He knew the only way churches all over the world would become genuinely healthy is for people to follow His example by "giving themselves up" for the church. This is the key difference between average and great congregations. Great churches are filled with people who love their church. This is the foundation and spirit of a correct ecclesiology (Matt 16:18; Eph 5:25-27, 29-32).

We must *seek and depend on divine moments.* Individual Christians never save anyone. It is only Jesus and the work of the Holy Spirit that save. We must learn to become better "workers together with God"

> **Great churches are filled with people who love their church!**

as He creates divine moments in people's lives. It is the presence of divine moments that determines basic church health. There is no relationship between church size and church health. Church health can occur, regardless of size. Healthy churches pray and hunger to experience divine moments where God is at work, transforming people's lives. God can do more in a five-minute divine moment that we can do in five years of organized church activity. (John 6:44, 15:5; 1 Cor 3:6-9, 13-15; 2 Cor 10:3-5).

We must *not depend on strategy, but on scripture.* The power to transform individuals and churches lies in using the Word of God. Church health and church multiplication must be driven by God's Word alone. While action planning, field research and human strategies are very important for our learning, we can never depend on them (Jer 17:5-8, 23:28-29; 1 Cor 2:1-5, 9-16; 1 Chr 12:32, 28:19).

We must *teach ReFocusing and corporate sanctification.* We describe ReFocusing as the process of moving a local church from being wrinkled toward becoming radiant. Jesus wants local churches both radiant and multiplying. This requires repentance, brokenness, renewal and the development of a sense of urgency to be different. The result of this attitude is not just individual but corporate sanctification, where all congregational decisions are driven by missional multiplication (Psa 51:17; Jer 24:7; 2 Chr 15:7; John 9:4, 12:24, 17:17-23; Luke 6:38).

> God can do more in a five-minute divine moment than we can do in five years of organized church activity.

Four Lessons from Church History

Effective ReFocusing movements emphasize the importance of having a correct, biblical view of the church. As Christians, we need a solid understanding of church history, both from a biblical as well as a historical perspective. We are then led to view the church as both local congregations and participants in spiritual movements. Here are four practical lessons we learn from church history as it relates to church health and church multiplication movements.

Lesson number one—*Paul was not a failure as a church planter and yet today, all the local churches the apostle Paul started do not exist.* Philippi, Corinth, Thessalonica and Ephesus are all examples. The local church Jesus started in Jerusalem that we read about in the book of Acts no longer exists. This certainly does not mean that Jesus or the apostle Paul were failures.

> ReFocusing requires repentance, brokenness, renewal and the development of a sense of urgency to be different.

Lesson number two—*God never intended local churches to be eternal, only the movement sustained by churches.* The ministry of the church always begins locally, but it can never stay there. Both Jesus and the apostle Paul had a vision that was much bigger than just one local church. If we follow their example, we will develop a similar vision.

Lesson number three—*local churches are just like people, in that they have life-cycles.* It is not a popular thought, but every person reading this book has a life-cycle. In the same way, churches are born, grow, mature, over time they plateau, decline, experience drop-out and die. The diagram on page 148 illustrates this reality. Parenting can occur anywhere along the life-cycle.

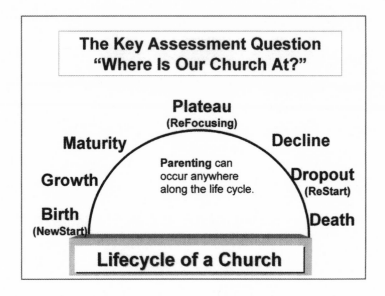

The main benefit in using the life-cycle diagram is for church assessment. The key assessment question is, "Where is our church?"

You will notice that NewStart churches are at the beginning of the life-cycle, ReFocusing churches are at the top side and ReStart churches are on the back side. There are many solid tools now available to assist congregations honestly committed to doing a church assessment.[1]

Lesson number four—*there is only one way for a church to avert the long-term results of the church life-cycle—regularly ReFocus its ministry.* This requires us to examine the ReFocusing process.

Understanding the ReFocusing Process

ReFocusing is the process of re-capturing the vision and heart of Jesus for His church—a radiant, healthy multiplying church. The process a church goes through in turning its focus away from itself to people who have not yet come is many times painful. Jesus regularly teaches throughout the gospels that if we want to save our lives, we must be willing to lose them (Mark 8:35). Paul teaches, "I have been crucified with Christ and I no longer live, but Christ lives in me. The life I live in the body, I live by faith in the Son of God..." (Gal 2:20).

The paradox of crucifixion is that only as we and our churches continually die to our own survival, do we maintain the momentum of a church health and church multiplication movement. The older a church gets, the more focused she becomes on self-survival. Many pastors deeply desire ReFocusing to happen where they serve, but the process to move from where the church is to where they desire the church to be is very difficult. Leading congregational change is a skill that can be learned, but it requires agenda harmony between pastors and key lay leaders to be successful.

> ReFocusing is the process of recapturing the vision and heart of Jesus for His church—a radiant, healthy multiplying church.

After evaluating and training hundreds of ReFocusing pastors, we have learned that ReFocusing is a process, not a pill. There is no quick fix. It is hard work and a pastor must have a clear focus to challenge his or her congregation to develop a sense of urgency to be different. This requires an adjustment of focus away from ourselves and onto the people outside God's grace who need to experience His love.

> The paradox of crucifixion is that only as we continually die to our own survival, do we maintain the momentum of a movement.

In her book *Reclaiming the "L" Word*, Kelly Fryer explains ReFocusing very clearly when she writes, "The church doesn't exist to meet my needs. It never did. Never will...God works miracles when those who have been set free by Jesus get caught up in what God is doing in the world and give themselves away. The church may be the only organization on the planet that exists entirely for the sake of those people who don't belong to it yet. In fact, as soon as we forget this and start making it all about ourselves, we stop being the church."[2] We have identified four main steps that churches take in the process of ReFocusing.

The first step is assessment. ReFocusing requires both an informal assessment of the pastor as well as a formal assessment of the church.[3] Not all pastors have the same kind of ReFocusing gifts, but every pastor leading an established church can benefit from learning the ReFocusing process. Church assessment involves doing a church health evaluation, life-cycle evaluation, historical and statistical analysis, core values audit, etc. all to determine the "current reality" of the church. A key role judicatories can play is in assisting pastors and local churches in the church assessment process.

The second step in ReFocusing is renewal. This includes both the personal renewal of the pastor and key lay leaders and the corporate renewal of the church. Repentance and brokenness before God are requirements. If a church is ReFocusing, it will have a "change of mind" and a "corresponding change of life." This is the biblical definition of repentance. The Bible's promise is, "Repent, then, and turn to God, so that your sins may be wiped out, that times of refreshing may come from the Lord" (Acts 3:19).

In launching the process of ReFocusing, many judicatories have spent an entire year renewing the spiritual life of their pastors. Being corrected by the Word of God and the Holy Spirit, developing a sense of urgency to be different, rekindling hope and passion — these are all crucial attitudes that must be present in ReFocusing churches. Every church has *gatekeepers*, people who have developed high levels of influence across the years. Many churches experience conflict between pastors and gatekeepers.

It is important to understand that in the Old Testament, gatekeepers were responsible to protect the people of God.

They were "the guards" who were cautious so Israel would not be harmed. In the new Israel of the church, we still have gatekeepers. These modern-day gatekeepers are often perceived as resistant to change and as obstacles to church progress. However, they have been created over time by the church's ministry. Every gatekeeper currently in place in a local congregation was at one time a new Christian and newcomer to the church. They gain influence over time because of their sacrifice and faithfulness to protect the church during pastoral transitions, financial crisis, conflicts and threats. Pastors must understand how gatekeepers develop and must learn to work with them. Gatekeepers must realize that the future existence of the church requires them to embrace ReFocusing so their church will not die but thrive.

> If a church is ReFocusing, it will have a "change of mind" and a "corresponding change of life."

The third step in ReFocusing is planning. ReFocusing churches must select a ReFocusing (vision) team and develop a Church Action Plan. This will require church leaders to learn new terms and receive specialized training. Judicatories are involved by linking ReFocusing pastors and churches together so they can learn from each other. The pastor and lay leaders must build the ReFocusing plan together. To be effective, ReFocusing requires gaining broad agenda harmony within the local church.

The fourth step in ReFocusing is implementation. Most pastors have been to at least 25 different conferences and have a shelf full of notebooks to prove it! At many conferences, information is given without a system of planning or implementation. Any effective church training requires a system of planning and accountability. Trained ReFocusing coaches are now emerging across North America. They understand the ReFocusing process, they

> Gatekeepers are responsible to protect the church. They gain influence over time because of their sacrifice and faithfulness.

are given a copy of the ReFocusing plan the pastor and leadership team have developed, and they assist the local church in implementing its ReFocusing strategies.

Hope for the ReFocusing Church

At an NCU presenter's meeting several years ago, my good friend Dan Croy gave us the following insights from the Scriptures about God's promise to the ReFocusing church. Thousands of churches in North America have known the glory of God in past days. They have good, godly, faithful people who look back and remember clearly what they believe were the church's greatest years.

To these wonderful people, God has a clear word. "Who of you is left who saw this house in its former glory? How does it look to you now? Does it not seem to you like nothing?" (Hag 2:3). This is exactly how people in churches who need ReFocusing feel. They are dwelling on the past and remembering the former years. They believe that if they simply do the things they once did, they will be able to resurrect their "former glory."

> While the people were refocusing on the past, God's real desire was for them to focus on the future.

But what does God declare to us through the prophet Haggai? Specifically to both leaders and people, God says, "But now...be strong, all you people of the land...and work. For I am with you...And my Spirit remains among you. Do not fear!" (Hag 2:4-5). "This is what the Lord says, 'In a little while I will once more shake the heavens and the earth...and the desired of all nations will come, and I will fill this house with glory.'" (Hag 2:6-7). In other words, while the people were focusing on the past, God's real desire was for them to focus on the future. They were looking backward when God wanted them to look forward. They needed the Messiah to arrive, and He wasn't behind them in the good old days—He was ahead of them and on His way.

God's promise to the ReFocusing church is that "'the glory of this present house will be *greater* than the glory of the former house,' says the Lord" (Hag 2:9). The greatest days we have as a church are not behind us; they are still ahead of us! The greatest gift of all from God to the ReFocusing church is when He says, 'And in this place I will grant peace'" (Hag 2:9).

God's promise of peace and the greater glory of His church does not mean that every local church will be ReFocused with outstanding numerical results. We are learning that sometimes the best strategy for church health is not to ReFocus but to ReStart. Congregations that are lower on the downhill side of the life-cycle are finding that in many situations, ReStarting the church can be a very effective outreach strategy.

11

ReStart, Church Closure & Corporate Sanctification

"I tell you the truth, unless a kernel of wheat falls to the ground and dies, it remains only a single seed. But if it dies, it produces many seeds."
John 12:24

Our purpose here is not to provide a comprehensive study of every issue affecting the ReStart process of a church, but simply to give an introduction to some of the key issues involved.

Understanding the ReStart Process

At NCS, we see the basic difference between a ReFocusing and ReStart church to be the involvement of judicatory leadership and the replacement of the church's governing board.

The factors that motivate a ReStart are many times a need to relocate and rename the church, a poor image or history in the community that must be overcome, and the need to remove unhealthy church power structures. Three biblical phrases articulated by Peter describe the process of ReStart. "Praise be to God…He has given us new birth into a living hope through the resurrection of Jesus Christ from the dead" (1 Pet 1:3). All ReStarts need a "new birth." They need "living hope" because their faith in a future being any different from the present has died. They need a "resurrection from the dead" because people who attend or visit sense the church is lifeless.

> Spiritual rebirth always includes a change of heart, a new beginning and a new life in Christ. Not just individuals, sometimes entire churches need this.

Jesus has been specializing in spiritual resurrections for the last 2000 years. Some have called it the rebirthing of the church and likened it to a church being "born again," or "born of the Spirit" (John 3:3, 5-6). Spiritual rebirth always includes a change of heart, a new beginning and new life in Christ. Not just individuals, but sometimes entire churches need this. A critical question is, "How does a church determine when it needs to ReFocus, and when it needs to ReStart?" The answer depends on where the church is at on the church life-cycle. The further the church is on the downhill side of the life-cycle, the more drastic the steps needed.

NCS has assisted many of our partners in implementing a ReStart process within their judicatory. A brief ten-step sample process is provided below as an example. The sample assumes an episcopal or representative form of church government, not congregational government.

1. Initiating the ReStart process is done after much prayer and analysis by judicatory leaders and the local church's governing board.

2. An intercession team from the church is mobilized for prayer throughout the process.

3. The entire ReStart process is communicated clearly to the congregation.

4. The local church governing board is dissolved, either by affirmative vote or judicatory action.

5. Local membership is dissolved and/or held by the judicatory.

6. All church programs and ministries are evaluated by judicatory leaders.

7. Judicatory leaders determine which programs continue to function and which ones cease.

8. A church planter is selected and a new Church Leadership Team is appointed by judicatory leaders.

9. The Church Leadership Team familiarizes itself with the resources that are available for ReStart churches. Team members attend training and prepare a ReStart Church Action Plan for judicatory or parent church approval.

10. Private Worship phase is begun, a ReStart Grand Opening date is set, planning of all future ministries is done, and the new church is launched.

Obviously each judicatory will need to contextualize its own policy and procedures for restarting churches. The policy must fit the polity structure of their denominational family or fellowship. There are multiple benefits of having a ReStart policy in place when a judicatory does a church assessment and is facing a ReStart situation. Communication between the judicatory leadership team and the church simply becomes a process of informing everyone of the decisions always made in these kinds of situations.

The policy protects denominational leaders from criticism because the decision is not being made personally by them, nor is the ReStart church being "singled out" while other churches are exempt. It saves time and money by providing guidance on how financial decisions will be made, as well as providing a step by step ReStart process for the church to follow.

Spiritual Attitudes about Church Closure

There are congregations on the downhill side of the church life-cycle all over North America that have a great history of faithfulness, where thousands of sermons have been delivered, tens of thousands of prayers prayed, Christian education classes have taught God's Word through the years, scores of people have been led to Christ, sacrificial giving to world missions has taken place, and where some have even been called into full-time ministry. What do we do in local church situations where the community changes, the church changes, the congregation ages and shrinks in size, the finances grow short and the church can no longer maintain its ministry?

From experience, we know the sacrifice of a previous generation has given many of these churches great assets. There are buildings and property, a great

> Each judicatory will need to contextualize its own policy and procedures for restarting churches.

testimony to past faithfulness. There is a spiritual legacy in every one of these churches that will never die, even if the church physically closes. The spiritual impact of that local church will live on throughout eternity. The people who are attending a church that seems to be nearing the end of its earthly days in ministry face some of the most difficult emotional feelings and hard decisions that anyone in a church ever faces. Their doctrine of the church and what they believe about the church is needed more now than ever before.

Even with ReFocusing and ReStart strategies, we are finding some church situations where church closure seems inevitable. It does not seem that the age, size, location and finances of the church will allow it to sustain its ministry. What should be done in such situations? The polity of the church's denominational connection greatly affects this.

My friend, Johnny Johnson, a Director of Mission for about 85 Southern Baptist churches in Louisiana, told me of some congregations that will not allow church closure or the selling of any building because of the graveyard covenants that tie the building to those buried beside it. In some places, even after they are dead, people still highly influence church decisions!

> The sacrifice of a previous generation has given many aging churches great assets.

What is the right attitude to have when a church faces a closure situation? In some congregations, the few remaining people begin to act very unspiritual. The walls go up, some people are driven to control, people are guided by protection and preservation instincts, there is a great struggle to maintain the status quo, an unholy passion develops to preserve church assets, and some people begin to demand "their rights."

There are other congregations who act very differently in these situations. They act spiritually. Prayers, not walls go up. The original vision of why the church was first begun is discussed. The congregation discusses the core values that spiritual churches have. The focus is not on preserving assets but rather on investing them. No one is demanding personal rights, because the model of behavior chosen is Jesus. He did not grasp for His rights but took on the nature of a servant and humbled Himself, becoming obedient even to death on a cross (Phil 2:5-8).

Corporate Sanctification Creates Multiplication

My good friend Joe Knight is the one who first introduced me to the concept of "corporate sanctification." This occurs when a church sacrifices part or all of itself for the greater multiplication of the Christian movement. It happens every time a church parents a new church. It also happens in church closure and church ReStart situations. It is vital we understand that theologically the kingdom of God is not crushed or defeated if a particular local church has to be closed or ReStarted. The multiplication movement of Christianity is much bigger than one local church or ministry. Our doctrine of the church calls us to acknowledge that what we are all part of is something bigger than ourselves. The person of Jesus Christ and the multiplication of the Christian movement is our common mission.

> The spiritual impact of every local church will live on throughout eternity.

At NCS, we have come to believe that church closure or church restarting is more than a strategy issue; it is a theological issue. How we close and ReStart churches is directly connected to our doctrine of the church and is fundamental to our doctrine of sanctification. There is a direct biblical relationship between sanctification and crucifixion. When I am crucified with Christ, my agenda no longer lives, but the agenda of Jesus is what drives my behavior (Gal 2:20). Let me reiterate the paradox of crucifixion. Only as we and our churches continually die to our self-interest and self-survival, do we maintain the momentum of a spiritual movement. Have you and your church been crucified? Do you, and does your church operate with a correct doctrine of ecclesiology toward church closure and restarting?

There was a time in most denominational families when both people and churches were "corporately sanctified." They were part of a movement that was bigger than they were. Sacrifice was common. Individual and corporate sanctification for the multiplication of Christ's church today are not just strategy issues or judicatory decisions. They are ultimately issues that reveal the spiritual attitudes of our hearts.

> It is vital that we understand theologically the kingdom of God is not crushed or defeated if a local church has to be closed or restarted!

The Metropolitan Church in Kansas City, Kansas, has had a great history of ministry. In the 1960's and 1970's, the church connected powerfully with the community around it. With a congregation of well over 350, they built and paid off a sanctuary seating 400, a full-size gym and fellowship hall, a beautiful brick parsonage, all sitting on ten acres of land. Across the years, the congregation aged and began to shrink. The community changed dramatically from Anglo to multi-cultural, with a primary concentration of African-American and Hispanic neighbors.

A new multi-cultural church called Risen Lamb was launched five miles away. This new church grew rapidly and filled the facility it was using. It desperately needed more space to grow. Pastor Ron Thornton, who served the Metropolitan Church, watched this new church with interest and began to pray about how the church could best meet the needs of the surrounding community. He and the Metropolitan church board reflected on their mission to reach the people around them who were culturally very different. After much discussion and many weeks of prayer, a motion was unanimously proposed by the church board to the congregation:

> "In order to continue to accomplish the original vision of the Metropolitan Church, we bestow our property to the Risen Lamb Church, believing that in so doing, they will carry on this great work to the glory of God!"

Following the pastor and the board's decision, the Metropolitan congregation voted to give their $1,500,000 property to the Risen Lamb Church to carry on the original vision of reaching their community. I was there when Pastor Ron Thornton walked across the platform, hugged Dorzell King, Jr, pastor of Risen Lamb, the new multi-cultural church and presented the keys of the entire property to him. That church building today is full of new people, community people, and the church of Jesus is moving powerfully ahead!

It is right for us to not only commend but also to make heroes of the Metropolitan congregation and Pastor Thornton. They voted to give all of their assets away so the church could multiply and go forward. This meant the pastor would have to relocate. When asked by the denominational leader, "What will you do if you give this church and this pulpit away?" Ron's reply was, "It's not about me, it's about what's best for God's church. God will take care of me."[1]

> Both individual and corporate sanctification are not strategy issues but issues of the heart!

This decision meant people giving up their pews, their shared history, their traditions and stepping into a new future. It meant becoming a home church fellowship[2] or finding another congregation in which to worship. Without question, it was the most difficult decision the Metropolitan church ever made. But it was the right thing to do. I was also present at the annual judicatory gathering where Dr. Keith Wright (denominational leader) recognized the small group from the Metropolitan church. In part, this is what he said to them:

> "This was the right decision for the Kingdom, for the church, for your community, and for you. God is already honoring your sacrifice and faithfulness. In a world where we are tempted

to control, to protect ourselves, to maintain the status quo and to preserve our assets, you have demonstrated our core value of what it means to be missional Christians. You have truly modeled what corporate sanctification is all about. Please know, God loves you, we love you, we appreciate you, and none of us here will ever forget your sacrifice and commitment."

Your Next Steps

Where is your church? What steps do you need to take to make your contribution to the Christian movement? A church health and church multiplication movement requires ReFocusing churches, churches that recapture the vision and heart of Jesus to be radiant, healthy multiplying churches. Churches that are truly ReFocused lock arms to become Parent and Sponsor churches willing to help NewStart churches. ReStart churches must be willing to sacrifice and take new risks to reach people in their community.

> They voted to give all of their assets away so the church could multiply and go forward.

Is God using anything you are reading to introduce you to new thinking? Will you consider letting God change the way you think? Is there anything God wants to renew in your mind by His Word so you can better gain His agenda? What would happen if we all came into harmony with the local church and judicatory leaders with which we serve, locking arms to create the vision Jesus has for His church, a church "like-minded, having the same love, being one in spirit and purpose?" (Phil 2:2). Do you desire to be part of a church health and church multiplication movement? If your heart is responsive, the movement has already begun where you live.

> Is there anything God wants to renew in your mind by His Word so you can better gain His agenda?

Part Three
Integrated, Healthy Church Multiplication

12

No Church Left Behind

"If you have any fellowship with the Spirit...
then make my joy complete by being like-minded,
having the same love, being one in spirit and purpose."
Philippians 2:1-2

At NCS, we focus greatly on the importance of momentum as it relates to launching a church health and church multiplication movement within a judicatory or denominational family. In his book, *The Unstoppable Force*, Erwin McManus talks about spiritual momentum and its relationship to lessons we can learn from the scientific world. "The formula for momentum is $P=MV^2$. P being momentum, M equaling mass, and V equaling velocity. Science understands momentum as the combination of mass and velocity squared."[1]

Building A Shared Vision

At an NCU in Phoenix, the insight of Daren Pitcher and John Volinsky fueled our learning even more in this area. Every church health and church multiplication movement requires momentum. Without a critical mass of individuals and churches, there is no momentum. The larger the mass, the larger the momentum we have. But mass is not enough;

we also must have velocity. Velocity is speed in a unified direction. A judicatory can have a group of people who share a vision, but it does not have movement momentum without critical mass and speed in a unified direction.

Agenda harmony is the key to gaining movement momentum. Every NewStart, ReStart, ReFocusing and Parent church is part of the critical mass needed. Pastors and lay leaders must see and understand the crucial role they play in the movement. The attitude must be developed that we want "No Church Left Behind." This is the process of building a "shared vision." Shared vision occurs when individuals and churches within a judicatory, denomination or fellowship begin to see themselves as a vital part of the health and multiplication movement.

Many people have asked the question, "Why do you put NewStart, ReStart, ReFocusing & Parent church training all together at New Church University? Why don't you segment your training and offer these different specialties at separate times?" There are two reasons we have chosen to go this direction. First, whether you are a NewStart, ReStart or ReFocusing pastor, writing a high quality Church Action Plan requires working through the 15 components to master the competencies of a solid plan.

Secondly, we have tried to practice what we preach about being a "learning organization." The moment we stop learning is the moment we stop leading. One of the lessons we have learned is that healthy judicatories, denominations and fellowships create "movement loyalty." We at NCS believe that part of our role is to teach individual and church loyalty to the judicatory, denomination or fellowship of which people are a part. All human expressions of the church are imperfect, but the church is God's only plan to bring salvation to the world. Only when we have loyalty and interdependent connectedness as God's church can we accomplish healthy church multiplication. Our teaching on "movement loyalty" makes NCS distinct from other training organizations and systems (Eph 3:10; Heb 13:17).

> A judicatory can have a group of people who share a vision, but it does not have movement momentum without mass and speed in a unified direction.

It is not just a few new churches, but a "critical mass" of NewStart, ReStart, ReFocusing and Parent churches that are necessary to launch and sustain a health and multiplication movement. Pastors and lay leaders must feel there is a vital place for them. The attitude we must create in every judicatory, in every denomination, in every fellowship is the attitude, "We care about you, we believe in you, and on our team there is help for you."

This principle is illustrated in the following e-mail from a pastor responding to an "Insights"[2] article on church health. He wrote, "I just wanted to let you know that your 'Insights' are being used by God to lift the spirits of at least one pastor. We have been working to restore a small church with a tragic history. In the past, I have been surrounded with the emphasis of plant, plant, plant new works. Without balance, this many times leaves me with a feeling that there is nothing for us established churches.

You have reminded me of the importance of everything God does, both small and large. As you focus on new churches, thanks for your concern in strengthening existing ones as well." This pastor said it perfectly. There is always a lot of excitement that surrounds having a baby, especially a baby church. We need them by the hundreds! But as a church planter or denominational supervisor, we can never forget the value and need for ReFocusing churches. We are in this together. Our commitment must be to help *every* church become a healthier church. In our movement, there must be "no church left behind."

> Healthy judicatories and denominations create "movement loyalty."

Becoming Process Driven, Not Program Driven

Healthy churches today do not just run programs or events…they design a clear process and system whereby they intentionally "make disciples." This is what we strongly emphasize and teach in helping every church create its ministry flow chart. In the same way, healthy judicatories and denominations do not just run programs or events…they design a *clear process* and *system* whereby church health and church multiplication is facilitated.

I will never forget working in Northern California a few years ago with twenty church leaders of a judicatory collectively building an integrated strategy. After the first session, John Calhoun, the judicatory leader, went to a white board and wrote the following: "Our system is perfect...for the results we are now getting. If we want different results, we must build a different system."

Integrated, Healthy Church Multiplication

We now have dozens of judicatories building an integrated process that is producing solid results. We call this *Integrated, Healthy Church Multiplication* (IHCM). The ten components of IHCM being developed and implemented by these judicatories are listed as follows:

1. **Judicatory Leader(s) Training.** We must orient denominational and judicatory leaders in their role of launching and sustaining a NewStart, ReStart, ReFocusing and Parent church movement of healthy churches. Specialized attention must be given to their role in ReStart as well as ReFocusing churches. Most districts, conferences, synods, associations, conventions, dioceses, presbyteries, regions, etc., are led not only

> We call our ten components of the IHCM system the 10 big rocks.

by the designated denominational leader, but also by a judicatory leadership team. These leaders have financial responsibility for assisting the judicatory in church planting, ReFocusing, Parenting, etc., but many times have little knowledge or standard procedures to follow. Every judicatory situation is different and calls for procedures that are contextualized to fit that judicatory. The education and training of the judicatory leadership team are a critical component in building an overall judicatory strategy.

2. **Agenda Harmony**. Pastors and key lay leaders in local congregations within the judicatory must work together for church health and church multiplication objectives, with a common purpose, in a common spirit. When this spirit is present, the church is unstoppable! We have learned that agenda harmony is a spiritual principle that must be taught to everyone within the judicatory.

3. **Recruitment**. Every healthy judicatory and denominational family must develop a "Farm System" for recruiting church planters. This requires the development of "spotters" on the campuses of educational institutions, as well as spotters in judicatories among people involved in pastoral credentialing. All NewStart, ReStart, ReFocusing and Parent church leaders need to work together within a system that identifies potential church planters three to five years in advance of their placement in the field. In chapter 15 we will talk more in detail about recruiting

the next generation of "apostolic" leaders.

4. **Assessment.** Every judicatory must use a high quality assessment process to ensure that only appropriately gifted individuals are placed in church planting situations. NCS uses the thirteen characteristics developed by Fuller Institute of Evangelism & Church Growth and Dr. Charles Ridley.[3] Effective ReFocusing also requires the assessment of pastors for appropriate placement. As a service to our partners who request it, NCS offers training to judicatory leaders in how to build their own assessment system. Included in the process is not just the assessment of leaders, but also tools for the assessment of local churches.

> Our system is perfect...for the results we are now getting. If we want different results, we must build a different system."

5. **NewStart Churches.** Every judicatory must have NewStart church planters who have been trained as new church specialists. They must master the details of new church development and develop a quality Church Action Plan that is regularly adjusted as the new church emerges. Because so much is at stake, we require every planter we train to secure a coach.

6. **ReStart Churches.** Every judicatory that has been in existence for over 75 years will have to involve itself

in ReStart church projects. While similar to NewStart churches in many ways, effective ReStart churches require judicatory involvement. They also require specialized training for the church planter to understand the unique issues normally faced by ReStart church leaders.

7. **ReFocusing Churches.** Healthy church multiplication ultimately flows out of ReFocusing congregations. This is a primary reason why judicatories must provide ReFocusing church training for existing pastors. We have already talked about the principles that guide ReFocusing churches in chapter 10.

8. **Parent Churches.** A church that is truly refocused has a desire to become a parent. Desire is not enough—there also must be knowledge and expertise. We must train Parent church pastors in the critical steps of parenting and how to develop effective Parent Church Action Plans. Every healthy judicatory church multiplication movement requires a growing number of parent churches.

9. **Coaching.** Once specialty training is provided, we have learned that effective NewStart, ReStart, ReFocusing and Parent church movements cannot be developed in pastoral isolation. Through trial and error, we have proven the critical role that coaching plays. The recruitment, training and maintaining quality assurance in the delivery of coaching to local churches are critical. Our long-term goal is for every judicatory

and denomination we work to develop its own group of nationally qualified coaches. We will deal with this issue in a later section.

10. **Church Health**—While attendance, dollars in the budget and church buildings are important, they are a very imperfect and incomplete way to measure the health of a local church. We use Natural Church Development as a church health evaluation tool.

> Effective ReFocusing also requires the assessment of pastors for appropriate placement.

We have found it to be stronger in diagnosis than prescription. Teaching and implementing church health principles in our training process provide a highly credible way of measuring the health of both large and small churches simultaneously. ReFocusing and ReStart situations especially require accurate church health evaluation.

The Ten Big Rocks

Stephen Covey relates the following story to illustrate the process of building both strategy and goals. A person has four containers. One holds sand, another holds water, another holds a group of large rocks and the fourth container is empty. The empty container represents our strategy and goals. If the objective is to get the sand, the water and the rocks successfully into the fourth container, it makes a big difference how they are put in.

If the sand is put in first, the water is put in second, and then an attempt is made to put the large rocks in, the objective will not be achieved. If, however, the big rocks are identified and put in first, then the sand poured in and then the water, the goal is met. The point of the story is this: in our strategic planning, we cannot begin with simply strategy and goals, the empty container. We must begin by identifying the big rocks.

> Every judicatory over 75 years old will have to involve itself in ReStart church projects.

At New Church Specialties, we have learned what the big rocks are in building church health and church multiplication movements. They are not new rocks; consultants and church leaders before us have identified similar stones. There are many great church health and church multiplication resources now available to judicatory and local church leaders. What is unique about our work is our learning related to the integration of the ten big rocks and how we use them to build agenda harmony within judicatories and denominational families.

Building Multiplication Movement Momentum

This leads us back to where we began this chapter. Every multiplication movement requires momentum. The scientific formula for momentum includes both mass and velocity.

We have pondered what a formula for "movement momentum" might look like and thought about the components. The following is where we are currently at in our thinking regarding the principles associated with it:

3M **= HS (AH + IHCM + CM)**

3M is Multiplication Movement Momentum

HS is the **Holy Spirit.** He alone creates divine moments that change people's hearts. It is ultimately His work alone that multiplies a church health and church multiplication movement.

AH is **Agenda Harmony.** Every movement requires it.

IHCM is **Integrated, Healthy Church Multiplication,** the ten components of an integrated system that healthy judicatories put in place.

CM is **Critical Mass.** There must be a sufficient number of pastors and laymen within the judicatory who share agenda harmony and begin creating the "anointing of unity."

In building multiplication movement momentum, we know it is the "anointing" of unity which is greater than any individual opinion (Eph 4:2). When church leaders leave personal agendas behind and lock arms for the common good of the movement, "the anointing of unity" leads to blessing beyond measure! We have learned the larger the judicatory mass and the more dispersed it is, usually the longer it takes to get a movement going. We have also discovered that an outside force is usually needed to get the judicatory mass moving. The good news is, however, once a "critical mass" is brought together and agenda harmony begins forming, the judicatory mass begins moving. If movement momentum is properly understood, inertia will keep the momentum going as long as the judicatory leader understands their role of always looking ahead and removing any barriers that may block progress.

Understanding the momentum of movements also requires the need to define the various groups of lay and pastoral leaders who are involved in either helping or hindering the momentum of a movement. "Adopters" are people who share the vision of church health and church multiplication. They seek agenda harmony with God and with those in leadership. In our work, we have discovered four clear groupings.

Early adopters: people who adopt the vision early on.

Mid adopters: people who adopt the vision once they see its progress through the participation of the early adopters.

Late adopters: people who adopt the vision only when they see the movement will be successful and not stopped by the no adopters.

No adopters: people who will never adopt the vision. Some people may actively resist, others may passively resist.

What leaders must understand about movement momentum is that a majority of people never share the vision when it is first cast. To begin a movement, you must start with a group of early adopters. They do not have to be large in number, but they must be people of influence within the church or judicatory if the movement is to enjoy beginning success.

> Our uniqueness is the integration of the 10 big rocks and how we build agenda harmony.

Shared vision within a movement always takes time to develop. "If it lingers, wait for it. It will come…" (Hab 2:3). While it normally begins with a leader, the movement only spreads when people "adopt" the vision for themselves and see their place in it. Once the early adopters begin sharing their excitement and commitment to the vision, the rest of the church or judicatory sits up and takes notice. As time goes on and progress is made, more people join the movement as mid adopters.

Everyone within the church or judicatory begin to sense a slow change of climate. What was once the prevailing attitude toward church health and church multiplication is slowly being readjusted. During the early adoption process is when many leaders are impatient and give up. For those who are persistent and able to gain agenda harmony with early and mid adopters, the movement thrives. In his best-selling book, *The Tipping Point*, Malcolm Gladwell describes what happens when an idea, a trend or a vision reaches a point of critical mass. After what has appeared to be a long push uphill, all of a sudden there is many times a "magic moment" when the vision crosses a threshold, tips and everyone involved experiences the impact of the movement. Agenda harmony is gained, even with late adopters, because everyone knows that the vision being shared will become a reality. It is no longer a question of "if," it is only a question of "when."

The church will be ReFocused, the church plant will launched, the parent church project will be successful, the painful steps toward church health will be taken, the judicatory will agree to adjust its priorities and the denominational decline in church planting will be reversed. All of these things are part of a vision, of a movement. Momentum toward achieving them with increasing regularity is what every church leader prays for.

New Church Specialties is not the only organization which delivers church planting, ReFocusing, Parent church and coach's training. There are several other good organizations who do similar work. There are multiple ways to build a church health and church multiplication movement. Even though our training, coaching and consulting system is integrated, it is not necessary that judicatories or denominations get all of their resource needs met from one source. Effective ministry in the 21st century will require many different kinds of church specialists. We have numbers of partners that have developed their own

ReFocusing process, but use NCS to train their parent churches and church planters. Other partners want only one or two specialties from us. While we do not believe we must be the ones to deliver all ten rocks to a judicatory partner for it to be effective, we do believe every judicatory leader must pay attention to implementing all of the rocks. All ten are critical in building a judicatory or denominational strategy.

> Momentum in a judicatory or denomination will do what $500,000 in the bank can never do!

We do not wish to imply that all judicatories and denominations should build an identical implementation strategy. How IHCM is implemented will depend on the polity structures of the various denominational families, the needs of each judicatory and how agenda harmony can best be gained in each setting. Our focus is making sure the big priorities are in place, key leaders are informed, agenda harmony is clearly understood, and the process of building momentum is begun. We have learned that momentum in a judicatory or denomination will do what $500,000 in the bank can never do! Our prayer is that within your judicatory or denomination, God will grant you His wisdom as you implement the big rocks and begin building momentum.

Part Four
Fueling the Movement

13
Intercession

"For our struggle is not against flesh and blood, but against the rulers, against the authorities, against the powers of this dark world and against the spiritual forces of evil in the heavenly realms."
Ephesians 6:12

Any church health and church multiplication movement requires fuel that will "fan into flame" (2 Tim 1:6) the work of God. As we have watched health and multiplication movements develop, it seems there are six different kinds of fuel that are required. Movements are fueled 1) through intercession, 2) through a commitment to multiplication, 3) through recruiting apostolic leaders, 4) through specialized training and resourcing, 5) through qualified coaches and consultants, and 6) through a worldwide vision and commitment. As we take a look at each of these six different fuels, our prayer is that God will quicken your heart to fuel the movement where you live and serve His church.

Can you imagine walking into a darkened room filled with people viewing a multi-media show—people who have never experienced anything other than darkness and the media illusion flickering before them? Imagine walking in, switching on the lights and asking everyone to turn around and look at the tiny little piece of equipment responsible for creating this powerful illusion that has deceived them for years. That is an analogy of what we as Christians face in dealing with our enemy. Satan is a projectionist, an illusionist, a deceiver and the father of lies (John 8:44). "The God of this age has blinded the minds of unbelievers, so that they cannot see the light of the gospel" (2 Cor 4:4). God has sent us as believers to open people's eyes so they can discover the truth about God, themselves, and the world. This kind of spiritual breakthrough can come about "only by prayer" (Mark 9:29). The following are seven biblical lessons we are learning about the impact of intercession on church health and church multiplication movements.

> "Prayer is far reaching in its influence and worldwide in its effects."
> —E.M. Bounds

Seven Biblical Lessons about Intercession

1. Intercession is directly connected to having clear spiritual sight. In fueling any church health movement, everything begins with the power of prayer. All of our New Church University training events begin with a session on intercession. We have dozens of Intercession Team members who pray constantly throughout the event. We believe E.M. Bounds when he writes, "Prayer is far reaching in its influence and worldwide in its effects. It affects all men, affects them everywhere, and affects them in all things. It touches men's interest in time and eternity." It is a powerful spiritual tool God uses to open people's eyes. Jesus said to Paul on the Damascus road, "I am sending you to open their eyes and turn them from darkness to light, and from the power of Satan to God, so that they may receive forgiveness of sins and a place among those who are sanctified by faith in me" (Acts 26:17-18).

There is a spiritual battle raging within your area and it is affecting you and your work right now.

Opening our spiritual eyes involves recognizing Satan's accusations and deceptions. "Be self-controlled and alert. Your enemy the devil prowls around like a roaring lion looking for someone to devour. Resist him, standing firm in the faith..." (1 Pet 5:8-9) You can be sure Satan will resist you and fight against you in your efforts to multiply Christ's church. Satan has two basic weapons he uses against believers—he accuses (Job 2:2-4; Rev 12:10) and he deceives (Gen 3:1-6). He hurls his accusations and lies with the greatest effect, not just in the secular world but also in the religious world. We must "resist him, standing firm in our faith" and when we do "he will flee from us" (Jam 4:7). Intercession is directly connected to having clear spiritual sight.

2. Intercession is directly connected to spiritual warfare.

All effective spiritual movements recognize the reality of an invisible spiritual war in which we are engaged. Paul says, "For our struggle is not against flesh and blood, but against the rulers, against the authorities, against the powers of this dark world and against the spiritual forces of evil in the heavenly realms" (Eph 6:12). We have learned that our multiplication effectiveness is directly linked to our living conscious of an invisible but very real spiritual conflict. One of the most dangerous things we can do in our work is to ignore this reality. Many Christians accept the Bible's teaching as true on this issue, but we often live our lives as though the battle existed on some far-off mission field, not in the town where we live. But the fact is, there is a spiritual battle going on in your area and it is affecting you and your work right now.

> "Whenever God determines to do a great work, He first sets His people to pray."
> —Charles Spurgeon

The great church leaders God has used throughout history all understood this invisible, spiritual war. They all confirm the power and need for effective intercession. Charles Spurgeon said, "Whenever God determines to do a great work; He first sets His people to pray." John Wesley wrote, "Give me 100 preachers who fear nothing but sin and desire nothing but God, and I care not a straw whether they be clergy or laymen, such alone will shake the gates of hell and set up the Kingdom of heaven on earth. God does nothing but in answer to prayer."

3. Intercession is a powerful spiritual resource. God uses it to prepare the person who is being led toward Christ. Prayer makes the people we pray for more open to the Holy Spirit and makes us more open to the Spirit's leadings as well. As we use the spiritual resource of prayer, people are more spiritually prepared to receive what we share with them. Jesus taught that prayer ties up the influence of Satan and releases the influence of the Spirit of God. "Whatever you bind on earth will be bound in heaven, and whatever you loose on earth will be loosed in heaven...if two of you on earth agree about anything you ask for, it will be done for you by my Father" (Matt 18:18-19). "Or again, how can anyone enter a strong man's house and carry off his possessions unless he first ties up the strong man? Then he can rob his house" (Matt 12:29). We most effectively use this spiritual resource when our spiritual armor is on (Eph 6:10-20).

> United prayer has a powerful impact in the process of gaining agenda harmony.

4. Intercession directly impacts agenda harmony. "When the day of Pentecost came, they were all together in one place" (Acts 2:1). It was prayer that preceded and prepared the way for Pentecost (Acts 1:14). The prayer of Jesus was for agenda harmony among all future believers:

"that all of them may be one, Father, just as you are in me and I am in you...May they be brought to complete unity to let the world know..." (John 17:21, 23). When a local church, judicatory or denomination sets aside the multiple agendas that regularly arise within the church and collectively seek the agenda of Jesus in achieving His Great Commandment and Great Commission, amazing things happen. United prayer has a powerful impact in the process of gaining agenda harmony.

5. Intercession builds our global vision. Every Christian has been given the Great Commission (Matt 28:19-20) Linked with it is the promise of Jesus that "all authority in heaven and on earth has been given to Him" (Matt 28:18). Because of Christ's authority, each of us has an opportunity and key role to play through prayer. When we are spiritually united and living in agenda harmony, the church of Jesus Christ is unstoppable! As Christ builds His church through efforts like planting, refocusing and parenting, we must regularly be reminded that our calling is always bigger than our own local area. As Great Commission Christians, we are contending for a whole generation, a whole planet! That is why God calls us to pray and act locally, but also to pray and think globally (Hab 2:14; Rev 11:15).

6. Intercession directly impacts church planter recruitment. Jesus taught this clearly "when He saw the crowds who were harassed and helpless, like sheep without a shepherd" (Matt 9:36). He said the solution was compassion and prayer. If we have a leadership shortage, we are to pray that God will send us the workers we need (Matt 9:38). In chapter 15, we will explain the clear relationship that exists between intercession and recruiting "apostolic" leaders.

7. Intercession directly impacts church multiplication. The model church in the New Testament for "worshiping the Lord and fasting" (Acts 13:2) was the church at Antioch. The spiritual climate the people created through intercession led naturally to healthy church multiplication. The whole atmosphere of church culture was bathed in prayer and dependency on the Holy Spirit. The Antioch church obviously had taken the words of Jesus to heart when He said to the disciples, "But this kind [of miracle, mountain-moving from God] does not go out except by prayer and fasting" (Matt 17:21). Through practicing the spiritual disciplines of prayer and fasting, the Antioch church put its members into a position where the Holy Spirit spoke and moved the church to powerfully multiply (Acts 13:3). The fuel of every church health movement includes intercession and prayer, which naturally leads to a commitment to church multiplication.

14

A Commitment
to Multiplication

*"While they were worshiping the Lord and fasting,
the Holy Spirit said, 'Set apart for me Barnabas and
Saul for the work to which I have called them.' So
after they had fasted and prayed, they placed their
hands on them and sent them off."*
Acts 13:2-3

For the last four thousand years of Judeo/Christian history, God's followers have been tempted to live solely by logic rather than by obedience and faith. The following are six biblical lessons we have learned as local congregations and judicatories become serious about the expansion and multiplication of God's church.

Six Biblical Lessons about Multiplication

1. Only what we give away multiplies. In the gospels, we see the disciple Andrew standing beside a little boy with a little lunch. The crowd around them is five thousand men, plus women and children. It does not make sense that Jesus and His disciples could take this little boy's lunch and make something happen with it. "Here is a boy with five small barley loaves and two small fish, but how far will they go among so many?" (John 6:9)

Here is a powerful reminder that when our resources are given away and placed in the hands of God, He can then take and multiply them. Jesus taught this basic spiritual principle in another way: "Unless a kernel of wheat falls to the ground and dies, it remains only a single seed. But if it dies, it produces many seeds" (John 12:24). When we are willing in the kingdom of God to take what we have and give it away, only then can it multiply.

There is an enormous temptation every congregation faces to focus only on addition—adding to our own local church or ministry. There is certainly a time for that. But when you begin seeing "your Jerusalem, Judea and Samaria" (Acts 1:8) the way Jesus sees it, you realize the task is far too big for one ministry or one local church. As you grow the kingdom where God has placed you, never forget what Jesus taught and modeled for us—only what we give away multiplies.

2. Multiplication is the key to feeding everyone. John 6:12 says, "they all had enough to eat..." As biblical Christians, we all have a deep passion to spiritually feed the world. Jesus is the bread of life (John 6:35). Our challenge is, "How do we get the bread to the people who need it?" Nowhere is this spiritual principle more relevant than in the area of multiplying new churches. When God gives us an assessed and trained NewStart or ReStart leader, and a parenting church takes a group of families and plants them in the work of extending the kingdom, something supernatural happens.

Many times giving people away is such a stretch—it seems so hard to let those families go. But when we as God's leaders obey Him, submit our own will and agenda, and give God's people away, it is then that God can take the people we have planted and multiply them—ten, twenty, thirty, fifty and sometimes even a hundred times what we sow (Matt 13:23). In the

> **Multiplication is the key to spiritually feeding everyone.**

gospel account, "everyone had enough to eat" because a little boy was willing to give away what he had to Jesus. Being willing to do that with the people and resources God has given us is the key to feeding everyone.

3. Jesus lived with a "next town" multiplication mentality. After beginning His ministry, Jesus knew He needed to consistently get away to experience spiritual renewal as well as to receive instruction from His Heavenly Father. After long days of healing and spending time with masses of people (Mark 1:33), Jesus needed direction. So "very early in the morning, while it was still dark, Jesus got up, left the house and went off to a solitary place, where He prayed" (Mark 1:35). The disciples came looking for Jesus; everyone else was looking for Him as well. In those early morning hours, Jesus received instruction from the Heavenly Father. "Whatever I say is just what the Father has told me to say" (John 12:50).

The direction of His ministry was made very clear. His Father wanted Him to have a "next town" mentality (Luke 4:43). Jesus had clear instructions, not just to plant the kingdom where He was, but also to plant it in the next town, among the next people group. Jesus was never content with planting His kingdom message in one location. As we study His ministry carefully, Jesus had what we call today an incredible "sponsor spirit." When His body, the church, commits to help sponsor a new church in another community or to reach another unreached people group, its members are following the spirit of Jesus we find here in the gospels. He said, "let us go somewhere else... this is why I have come" (Mark 1:38). Jesus had a clear "next town" multiplication mentality.

4. God expects cooperation and interdependence to characterize His church. In the history of Israel, there were people filled with both fear and faith (Num 13:25-32). God had given them the promise of taking the Promised Land. Moses told them, "The Lord your God has given you this land to take possession of it. But all your able-bodied men, armed for battle, must cross over ahead of your brother Israelites...until the Lord gives rest to your brothers as He has to you, and they too have taken over the land that the Lord your God is giving them, across the Jordan. After that, each of you may go back to the possession I have given you" (Deut 3:18, 20).

For biblical Christians, the Old Testament typology here is clear. God wants us to learn lessons from Israel's history, both bad and good. "These things happened to them as examples and were written down for us" (1 Cor 10:11). Assisting our brothers in taking new territory is not a suggestion. It is God's command. The tribes on the east side of the Jordan had already received their inheritance. But God did not want them to settle down in comfort. There was more territory to conquer. God wanted established leaders to be involved in the "taking new territory" process. He expected a spirit of cooperation and interdependence among His people.

> Jesus was never content with planting His Kingdom message in one location.

His promise to His people was clear. "The Lord has *given us* territory to take possession of it" (Deut 3:18). God had promised territory multiplication! However, there was only one way for that to happen. "All your able-bodied men, armed for battle," in other words, the existing spiritual army, must be willing to cross over ahead of God's expanding work. The principle is crystal clear. God expects everyone to cooperate. He is calling everyone to be co-laborers with Christ. We must survey the land and we must bring back a report, not of doubt but of faith.

God's plan is that before any NewStart, ReStart or ReFocusing churches settle into the comfort of their "own land" that has been safely possessed, they must maintain a spirit of interdependence. We must have movement leaders who willingly lead the way as Parent churches, cooperating to multiply God's church. We all must work together "until the Lord gives rest to our brothers" just as He has given rest to us (Deut 3:20). God expects a spirit of cooperation and interdependence to reign among us as we lock arms to extend His kingdom.

5. New churches must commit to multiplication before they begin. As we have trained hundreds of church planters, we have watched many of them on the receiving end of parent church sacrifice. Jesus taught, "It is more blessed to give than to receive" (Acts 20:35). This is why at New Church University, we require church planters to sign a commitment that they will help parent or sponsor a new church within the first three years following launch.

> God expects cooperation and interdependence among Christians.

We expect cooperation, interdependency and loyalty to the judicatory, denomination or fellowship that is birthing them.

Many planters attend NCU without money, members, a building or other resources that they can count on as they begin. Do we ask them to make this same commitment to multiply within the first three years following launch? The answer is yes. We have learned that church multiplication is not a members or money issue. It is a heart issue. God's kingdom does not need more independent, maverick-minded planters doing their own thing. Every judicatory and denomination needs hundreds of loyal, multiplication-minded leaders who see the world and have made a life commitment to link arms together and cooperate in taking the world for Christ.

If you are in a new church, you must cooperate and be loyal in assisting the particular church multiplication movement that birthed you. A new church must decide from the beginning never to become ingrown, but rather to help multiply new churches until every unchurched person yet to be spiritually fed throughout the world may finally sit down and eat.

6. We must focus on creating a spiritual climate that produces parent churches. The church at Antioch had a clear multiplying, global mission. It was not a church filled with Jewish Christians who had simply migrated from their home church in Jerusalem and were content to remain to themselves. Instead, the church was begun by the work of "men from Cyprus and Cyrene" (Acts 11:20) who "had been scattered by the persecution in connection with Stephen" (Acts 11:19). They had gone to Antioch and began witnessing to Greeks about Christ. Out of their efforts, a church was born, and when the Jerusalem church heard about it, Barnabas was sent down to encourage them and oversee the work (Acts 11:22-26).

Church leaders already knew that not every person who needed Christ would join the Antioch church. They already realized that the measure of a great church was not its seating capacity but its sending capacity. They understood what Paul later wrote, "How can they believe in the one of whom they have not heard? And how can they hear without someone preaching to them? And how can they preach unless they are sent?" (Rom 10:14-15) It was in an atmosphere of worshiping the Lord and fasting that the Holy Spirit spoke about releasing two key leaders as the first official church planters of the Christian faith (Acts 13:2).

The spiritual climate of the Antioch church produced a parent church. Its members were sensitive, prepared and ready for obeying anything the voice of the Holy Spirit would tell them to do. They are the New Testament model for parent churches worldwide. They had agenda harmony and the spiritual climate was right. The church was obedient and the result was a parent church sending service. "So after they had fasted and prayed, they placed their hands on Barnabas and Saul and sent them off" (Acts 13:3).

> We require church planters to sign a commitment that they will help parent or sponsor a new church within the first three years.

Notice the way Antioch acted as a New Testament parent church. Here we discover a model for how a Parent Church sending service can be conducted. There were the elements of fasting, prayer and the laying on of hands. The Antioch church members gathered around Paul and Barnabas and, laying their hands on them, they communicated to them personally their love, support and deep, genuine care. As a parent church, never underestimate the value of a word or touch. Church planters being sent out by parent churches need to feel emotionally loved with the same kind of spiritual atmosphere that was clearly present at Antioch. Then they will more aptly return with joy in reporting how God has "opened the door of faith" (Acts 14:27) for the people to whom He has sent them.

God wants every church today to experience what happened in the early church. God wants hundreds of local churches to sponsor

> We must focus on creating a spiritual climate that produces parent churches.

and parent new churches, just like the church at Antioch did. If judicatories and denominations focus on creating a spiritual climate that produces parent churches, they have the promise that God will certainly open many new doors of faith! (Acts 14:27)

15

Recruiting Apostolic Leaders

"Then I heard the voice of the Lord saying,
'Whom shall I send? And who will go for us?'
And I said, 'Here am I. Send me!'"
Isaiah 6:8

Every multiplication movement requires God to raise up and provide hundreds of apostolic leaders for the church. This reality is powerfully communicated in the book by Episcopal Bishop Claude Payne, *"Reclaiming The Great Commission."* Bishop Payne correctly contends that the church must enter the New Apostolic Age by recovering the characteristics of the First Apostolic Age. [1] When Christianity first came to America and spread, it had apostolic characteristics and was apostolically driven.

The Development of American Christianity

The historical development of American Christianity is a powerful example of how apostolic leaders were recruited. In 1750, the Baptists in America had a total of 180 churches. By 1792, they had become the largest denomination in America. During this record rate of growth, they got the job done primarily by apostolic bi-vocational church planters who shared their faith and started churches, primarily throughout the south.

By 1820, the Methodists had more churches than the Baptists. Methodism came to America in the 1760's, and because of its church planting methods, it soon became the largest Protestant denomination in America. The secret of its outstanding growth was scores of apostolic church planters who were sharing their faith and starting churches. A hundred years following the American Revolution, it was clear that the two largest religious bodies in America would be the Baptists and the Methodists. The reason for the growth of both denominations was their use of hundreds of "apostolic" church planters. The basic principles used in their growth were identical, but their methods differed greatly.

> The reason for the growth of both Methodists and Baptists in America was their use of hundreds of "apostolic" church planters.

The Methodists impacted the expanding frontier of America and planted churches with what became known as the "circuit rider." The circuit rider was usually not a college-educated, but self-educated preacher with spiritual influence, whose natural leadership sprang up from within the Methodist study groups, called societies. With a burning passion and a divine call to fulfill, the Methodist circuit riders rapidly covered the country, paying the price to fulfill the Great Commission.

The Baptists had a different philosophy and method of planting new churches on the frontier, but with similar success. Rather than having a traveling lay-pastor like the circuit rider, most Baptist preachers emerged out of the community. They were usually self-educated farmers with a call to preach. They were radically committed to preaching the salvation message they found in the Bible and establishing the church in their community. Because of their zeal for Christ and their participation in the culture they were reaching, their witness and leadership in planting churches was usually more effective than the leadership of professionally trained clergymen coming out of eastern cities. American church history teaches us that the two largest denominations in America became great as a direct result of their apostolic evangelizing methods.

If we had time and space to examine the history, we would find that Lutherans, Presbyterians, Episcopalians, Christian churches, Reformed churches, any mainline movement that flourished by multiplying new churches, had apostolic leaders. As America developed, numbers of new denominational families emerged to fulfill the multiplying mission of Christ's church. Without exception, every effective spiritual movement and resulting denominational family or fellowship had at its center and heart a vast array of apostolic, church planting leaders. We contend that the only way spiritual movements and denominational families will flourish in the 21st century is by the church recognizing and continuing to "send out" hundreds of new apostolic leaders.

Apostolic Gifts Needed Today

Whether we call the church planting gifts the spiritual gift of apostle, or the gift of missionary, or by some other name, the title is not important. What is important is that we recognize the apostolic work of Christ continues and that Jesus is still giving and wants to give apostolic gifts and a divine call to persons being "sent out" by the church. I personally believe an in-depth study of the scriptures on this issue reveals that the gift of apostle (or apostolic ministry) *did not* die out in the early church. I want to *un-dogmatically* suggest that the gift of apostle is a spiritual gift that God gives to an individual to go where a new church is needed and cooperate with the Holy Spirit in digging out a new body of Christ.[2]

> The only way spiritual movements and denominational families will flourish in the 21st century is by recognizing and sending out hundreds of new "apostolic" leaders!

As we study the scriptures, we find clear biblical support for this idea. The word "apostle" [apostolos] or "apostles" occurs eighty-five times in the New Testament. Many Christians today have a limited understanding of the word apostle because five times in the gospels the twelve disciples of Jesus are referred to as "apostles." There is no doubt the Twelve were a unique group that will never be added to. But in later parts of the New Testament, the use of the term "apostle" is much more broadly understood than simply in reference to the Twelve.

There are at least seven other persons who are called apostles in the New Testament. Just to mention a few, the New Testament names Barnabas (Acts 14:14), Paul (Rom 1:1), Andronicus and Junias (Rom 16:7), Apollos (1 Cor 4:6, 9), James, the brother of Jesus (Gal 1:19), Silas and Timothy (1 Thess 1:1, 2:7), as those who were listed among the apostles of the church. First Corinthians 15 mentions that after the resurrection, Jesus appeared to "the Twelve" and then also to "all the apostles," indicating there were apostles other than the Twelve (1 Cor 15:5, 7). Also, the warnings against "false apostles" would be nonsense if apostles in the early church were limited only to the Twelve. In both 2 Corinthians 11:13 and Revelation 2:2, references are made to these "false apostles," indicating that in the ministry of the early church, there were certainly more apostles than just the Twelve.

This raises the question, "Who were the apostles beyond the Twelve in the New Testament?" The word apostle simply means, "one who is sent." We believe then and now that people continue to be sent out by Christ and His church to dig out new works in the extension of the Kingdom. The gift of apostle is always mentioned first in the listing of spiritual gifts (1 Cor 12:28; Eph 4:11) because it is the most essential gift given to begin God's church. If there is no apostle sent, there is no church! It is the exercise of apostolic gifts that allows all of the other gifts to effectively operate within a healthy church body.

The gift of teaching and pastor and mercy and giving and all the other gifts listed are made possible because we, first of all, have a church. Our prayer is that God will grant the church a fresh, new awareness for the need of "apostolic gifts" to be recognized and released in our day. We believe the multiplication of God's church depends on Christ continuing to give "some to be apostles" (Eph 4:11). We would never suggest or imply replacing the Twelve — we simply seek to emulate the "sending spirit" of the New Testament church (Acts 13:2-3). Scripture, reason, tradition and experience in the history of Christianity all confirm this.

> It is the exercise of apostolic gifts that allows all of the other gifts to effectively operate within a healthy church body.

As a pastor, judicatory or denominational leader seeking these "apostolically gifted" individuals, sometimes it is easy to get so caught up in our need for church planters that we forget what Jesus taught us to do when we have a leadership shortage. He did not say we should panic or pout. He clearly instructed us to pray. It is intercession, "asking the Lord of the harvest to send out workers into His harvest field" (Matt 9:38) that fuels the process of God raising up the leaders needed for His church to effectively multiply.

We have seen it happen over and over again within judicatories, denominations and fellowship families. Church planting leaders are needed. A vision is cast and the need is identified. People get serious and start to pray for God to raise up leaders for a mighty multiplying harvest. As a result, God begins to reward our dependence on Him to build His church. "Apart from me, you can do nothing" (John 15:5). Looking to the Lord of the harvest for new leaders keeps us regularly dependent on Him for what He alone can do.

Do you sense a call to lead or participate in a new church? As you read this, are you feeling that Christ may want to send you? (Isa 6:8) The greatest opportunity and privilege in the world is to be involved in multiplying Christ's church. Today, you can begin the process of joining the ranks of the apostle Paul and be able to say with him, "(your name), called to be an apostle of Christ Jesus by the will of God" (1 Cor 1:1). If you are "sent by Christ and His church," you are functioning in a truly apostolic way, using apostolic gifts. The church needs you now more than ever!

Planter Recruitment & Tracking

To help you assess whether you have the gifts and skills necessary to plant a new church, under the Assessment section at NCS on the Web (www.NewChurchSpecialties. org), you will find our Church Planter Self-Assessment

Guide. This will help you identify the thirteen characteristics effective church planters have. There you can do a beginning assessment. At NCS, we also assist local church, judicatory and denominational leaders in achieving their planter recruitment objectives. We have a Church Planter Tracking Process we have developed over the past several years that we offer to our partners for their use.

> Looking to the Lord of the harvest for new leaders keeps us regularly dependent on Him for what He alone can do.

The process begins when a referral conversation or contact takes place, which identifies a person as a potential church planter. We have learned this referral happens through one of several ways. Referral may come through a church planter, a pastor, a lay leader, a judicatory leader, a college or seminary "educational spotter," a denominational leader or from NCS on the Web. Once referred, basic information about the potential planter is gathered and entered into a recruitment database.

The Planter Recruitment Coordinator sends a follow-up e-mail to the potential planter, which includes helpful beginning information. If desired, we also have a phone appointment with the potential planter, answering basic questions about the church planting process. We identify when the potential planter would be available for assessment, if he or she has interest in any particular location or judicatory, and following assessment, when he or she would be available to plant.

The Planter Recruitment Coordinator maintains contact with prospective planters through Assessment, New Church University training, placement and provides support until they are handed off to a qualified coach. For ease of tracking, we identify potential planters and move them through five different tracking levels.

Tracking Level #1 is the **Entry Level**. These are potential planters who are highly interested in planting but need four or five years of education, mentoring and experience. They may be young ministerial students or in a second career.

Tracking Level #2 is the **Experienced Level**. These are potential planters who have solid ministry experience. They and the people who know them believe they may be ready to plant. However, they are two to three years away from finishing their education, completing a ministry assignment or some other obligation.

Tracking Level #3 is our **Assessment-Ready Level**. These are potential planters who are less than two years away from placement. They may currently be pastors, church staff, lay leaders, students, etc. They have a good ministry background and are ready for a formal assessment.

Tracking Level #4 is our **NCU Level**. These are planters who have passed a formal or informal assessment and are either ready for New Church University or have already completed it. They feel clearly called by God to plant a new church in a specific location and are developing a Church Action Plan for presentation and feedback.

Tracking Level #5 is our **Coaching Level**. These are planters who have been placed and are now in the coaching and implementation phase of their planting project.

> For ease of tracking, we identify potential planters in one of five different tracking levels.

As NCS expanded its role in planter recruitment, one of the key issues we had to clarify was the development of a policy with our NCS Partners in how we handle the "judicatory/ movement loyalty" issue. As we now work with hundreds of potential church planters from multiple judicatories and denominations, we must protect the quality of our service to each NCS Partner and their vested interest in the church planters they have entrusted to us.

As a result, NCS established what we call our "judicatory/movement loyalty" policy regarding church planters. Our Judicatory Partners have regular access to all information on persons connected with them. A personal contact is made by NCS to the judicatory when an individual from that judicatory is added to our tracking system. (The only exception to this would be if for some reason the potential planter asks that his or her name be kept confidential for the time being.)

All NCS tracking information is totally confidential and will not be given out to anyone except the Judicatory

Partner with whom the planter has an established working relationship. If a potential planter has notified his or her judicatory in advance of the intention to talk with other interested sponsors or has clearly communicated with NCS that there is no binding relationship with that judicatory, we then move that potential planter to our "available for placement" list. As the NCS Recruitment system matures and our number of available planters increases, we hope to link large numbers of Level 3 & Level 4 planters with our Judicatory Partners. In a number of cases, this has already occurred.

On page 218, you will find the ten-step **NCS Tracking Funnel** that we use in helping church planters move through the entire planting process. In using the image of a funnel, the grey dots represent potential church planters entering the top of the tracking funnel. There is a much larger group of people at the top end, but as potential planters move through the entire process, there is a smaller group of "placed planters" at the lower end. You will notice the bottom of the funnel is positioned for church planters to be produced and placed throughout the world.

Each box on page 218 represents and explains a distinct step we have developed—from initial planter identification and recruitment to securing a qualified coach, building a launch team and executing a Church Action Plan. Our purpose here is to explain how NCS assists judicatories, denominations and potential planters to determine God's call on their lives and move through the entire planting process. For more information, we

NCS Tracking Funnel

1. Identification & Recruitment

1. Interest & contact is made with the potential planter through several avenues: judicatory leaders, pastors, planters, educational spotters, NCU attendees, NCS on the Web, etc.

2. NCS determines potential planter's current situation, interest, time frame for planting & places planter in the appropriate recruitment level. (Levels 1-5)

2. Placement in Appropriate Level

3. The potential planter is connected with a mentoring pastor or planter for on-going development & support. Education in the planting process is provided in multiple ways.

3. Mentoring & Education

4. NCS provides Pre-Assessment tools & training to our Partners to assist in determining basic church planting capability, experience, spiritual gifts, abilities, etc.

4. Pre-Assessment

5. Most judicatories & Parent churches require either a 3 day Assessment Center or 1 day Behavioral Interview to formally evaluate planter & spouse capabilities, background, skills, etc.

5. Formal Assessment

6. A 3-day training/workshop event where the potential planter is equipped with tools & training necessary to develop a quality New Church Action Plan.

6. New Church University

7. This is done by a Parent Church pastor and/or Judiciary leader. The potential planter is informed of the appropriate policies & procedures in planting the new church in the selected location ---varies by church / judicatory.

7. Expectations Interview

8. A formal presentation of the New Church Action Plan is given by the planter & final approval is agreed on for the planting project.

8. Project Approval

9. NCS provides multiple levels of coaches training & qualification. We HIGHLY RECOMMEND no planter proceed without securing a coach.

9. Secure A Qualified Coach

10. Planter establishes the launch team, seeks parent/sponsor churches, raises support & executes the plan (adjusting as they go!)

10. Build Launch Team & Execute Plan

encourage you to visit the Recruitment & Tracking section of NCS on the Web.

We are totally committed to partnering with judicatories, denominations and fellowships so that annually hundreds of qualified, apostolic leaders will be identified, recruited, mentored, assessed, trained and effectively coached throughout the world. This leads us to the next source of fuel required for a church health and church multiplication movement—specialized training and resourcing.

16
Specialized Training & Resourcing

"Everyone who competes in the games goes into strict training. They do it to get a crown that will not last; but we do it to get a crown that will last forever."
1 Corinthians 9:25

Every church health and church multiplication movement in the 21st century will require specialized training and resourcing. Evangelism Explosion Training teaches, "It is more important to train a soul winner than it is to win a soul." In adapting this to a church health and church multiplication movement, "It is more important to train a church planter than it is to plant one church. It is more important to train a ReFocusing pastor than it is to ReFocus one church."

Winning one person to Christ can be likened to picking an apple. Training a church planter or ReFocusing pastor for effective outreach can be likened to planting an apple tree and harvesting bushels of apples. Multiplying and training dozens of church planters and ReFocusing pastors within a healthy, multiplication movement can be likened to planting entire orchards! Dr. Chic Shaver taught me there is a huge difference between addition and multiplication in ministry and our God is into multiplication big-time! This kind of multiplication requires specialized training.

Solving Problems Concerning Training

The clear way to gain leadership in any circumstance is to tackle and begin solving problems that large numbers of people collectively face. It took sixteen years of preparation before God led us to launch New Church University. I wish I could tell you that NCU was a dream I had for years, but it was not. The specific details and learning really did not begin taking shape until the fall of 2000. Years ago, however, although our first church plant did moderately well by some standards, it was easy for me to realize that as a church planter, I had no earthly idea what I was doing. As a result, as we moved from our first church plant into the second, I vowed to God that if I did not do anything else with my life, I would commit to change the way the church trains people to start and multiply churches.

> We will always be frustrated if we try by willpower and effort to do something that is only possible for those who train.

Through a personal journey too long to tell, the vision has emerged to include NewStart, ReStart, ReFocusing and Parent churches. I have come to believe with all my heart that before I was born, I was chosen by God for this work (Jer 1:5). Even though it has taken and in the future may take several forms, this is my life mission.

I believe I was chosen to fulfill this calling, just as clearly as a man or woman is chosen by God to go to a foreign country as an overseas missionary or chosen to work among the poor of the inner-city. God in His sovereignty—I have no other

> It was easy for me to realize that as a church planter, I had no earthly idea what I was doing.

way to explain this but sheer sovereignty—chose me to do what I am doing and prepared me for it through events and circumstances so far beyond me and in ways that are so much higher than my ways (Isa 55:9).

Because of my own personal journey, numerous failures and much trial and error learning, at NCS we are radically committed to the power and importance of high quality training. We know this is a critical component to fueling a church health and church multiplication movement. We must provide specialized training and resourcing to every church leader we can serve throughout the world who feels God's call.

Trying Versus Training

One of the lessons we have learned is that, in the ministry, there is a *huge* difference between *trying* to do something and *training* to do something. On several occasions the New Testament writers use athletic metaphors. They address this key issue: "How can I put myself in a position where I can be empowered by the Holy Spirit for maximum effectiveness?" Paul answers by writing, "Do you not know that in a race all the runners run, but only one gets the prize? Run in such a way as to get the prize. Everyone who competes in the games goes into strict training..." (1 Cor 9:24-25).

The point is that effective athletes focus. They practice discipline and they train. The image Paul offers us is of Olympic-type games. On the day you are reading this book, there are athletes worldwide who got up this very morning and trained ten to twelve hours. They will do that tomorrow and the next day, training six days a week for four years, just for twenty seconds on an international stage. If they miss the mark by 1/10th of a second, the world hardly even notices them. If they win the gold medal, the chances are good someone else will win four years later and take their crown.

Paul sees the reality of all this and writes, "They do all this to get a crown that will not last; but **the training we put ourselves through** is for a crown that will last forever" (1 Cor 9:25). We see Paul use a similar athletic metaphor with the added admonition, "train yourself to be godly. For physical training is of some value, but godliness has value for all things, holding promise for both the present life and the life to come" (1 Tim 4:7-8).

We want to suggest there is a critical distinction these athletic metaphors make—the distinction between *trying* to do something and *training* to do something. We will always be frustrated if we try by willpower and effort to do something that is only possible for those who train. Millions of people in North America focus on reaching their physical potential through exercise and conditioning. They join health clubs and watch people demonstrate in those clubs what the human body can become. They have devoted themselves to training and health. The habits of their lives, what they eat, how they exercise, how they rest, are devoted to the task of developing health and getting into good physical condition.

Such a process is not easy to follow nor is good physical condition easy to achieve. If you do not have the habits of physical conditioning, can you go to a health club and immediately begin to compete with others by simply "trying really hard?" Are desire and willpower alone enough? The answer is no. The fact is, you cannot compete because you have not *trained* to do so.

If you are serious about physical conditioning, you will have to enter into a life of training. *You will have to arrange your life around activities that enable you to do by training what you cannot now do by trying.* Paul is making the point that this is the way life works in every area. Training enables us to do what we can never do by trying.

Now let's bring Paul's teaching here into the church realm. Across the years, many lay and clergy leaders in the church have experienced enormous frustration because they have focused on trying instead of training.

This brings us into the whole issue of spiritual disciplines. A spiritual discipline is "a spiritual activity that, when practiced, will help me do what I cannot now do by direct effort." It requires time and training.

As an example, this includes the discipline that surrounds spiritual strategic planning. Learning and being trained in how to spiritually plan takes church leaders far beyond their own efforts in trying to make the church different.

It is not any human planning activity that transforms us or the church. God is the only One who transforms. But God uses these kinds of spiritual activities and disciplines to put us into a position where He can work. We are then able to do by training what we can never do by trying.

Do you remember the section entitled, "The Huge Impact of Our Thinking?" How we think leads to how we act. How we act determines the habits we form. The habits we form determine our character, and our character determines our destiny. *Good habits, in people as well as in churches, are formed by training.* This is why we are radically committed to the ongoing development and delivery of a quality training process.[1]

21st Century New Church "Specialties"

At this juncture in church history, we believe hundreds of judicatories, denominations and fellowships stand poised and ready like a giant rocket ship on a launch pad, experiencing countdown. God is right now in the process of pulling together all of the resources needed to thrust them from their present position into orbit toward their church health and church multiplication objectives. Dozens of denominational and fellowship families are now beginning to communicate a clear commitment for the future that includes church health and church multiplication.

The mandate and call is crystal clear. What is needed is the fuel for lift-off into orbit. The church is poised and ready to be launched into a 21st century multiplication ministry. The question is, who are the persons who will lead the church into her future? Who will push the button? Who will direct the charge? Who will launch the ship?

We believe the answer is not just judicatory

> The future of the 21st century rests in the hands of a new army of apostolic NewStart, ReStart, ReFocusing and Parent church leaders God is raising up.

or denominational leaders, although they have a vital and important role to play. We believe the future of the church in the 21st century rests in the hands of a new army of apostolic NewStart, ReStart, ReFocusing and Parent church leaders God is raising up. Seminaries and Christian colleges do a great job of training pastors in Bible, history, doctrine and church government. *Their foundational role is critical and we must have it continue with excellence.* But ministry in the 21st century is going to require more than this foundational pastoral training. We believe it will require training in new church "specialties" that are specific and unique to particular church settings.

History has taught us that effective church planters must be recruited, mentored, educated, assessed, trained and coached. ReFocusing and Parent church leaders must be provided unique specialty training and coaching as well.

The future of church health and church multiplication movements rests in our ability to marshal the human and material resources we need to achieve our objectives. We believe this is one of the reasons God has caused New Church Specialties and other similar organizations to come into being.

Our vision is that one day every NewStart, ReStart, ReFocusing and Parent church will have all of the training and resourcing they need to perform the specialty task God has given them. Our vision is that their character, competence and confidence will rise along with their leadership, as they write and execute high quality Church Action Plans.

Because we believe the principles we teach at NCU are trans-cultural, we are committed to refining and contextualizing their use not only in North America but also worldwide. Our vision is to positively contribute to the way every church leader is trained, both here in America and around the world.

How a Pastor's Dream Changed America

We are not the first to tackle massive improvements

in specialty education and training. Back in 1890, a pastor named Frank Gunsaulus began his preaching ministry in the stock yards region on the south side of Chicago. After several years in the ministry and also rubbing shoulders with education, he began to realize there were huge defects in the educational system in America, defects that affected numerous students. Frank Gunsaulus believed he could help correct those problems if he were made the head of a college. God began to develop in him a burning desire to become the directing head of an educational institution where young men and women could "learn by doing."

The question was, how would God do it? The year was 1890, and Pastor Gunsaulus estimated he would need at least a million dollars to put the project into operation. That was a lot of money back then and even today. How could he ever come up with that kind of cash? He certainly did not have it and neither did his congregation. But Frank Gunsaulus lived with his dream of a new college for so long that it became an unshakable conviction. He believed this was exactly what God wanted him to do.

He did not know how he would ever get the money for the project, but he simply laid out his plans and believed that if God was in it, if God had given him the desire, God was also big enough to give him the money. He believed so strongly that God wanted this college that his prayer and planning went on for months and months in his life. From his own account, this is how God brought about the outcome.

"One Saturday afternoon I sat in my room thinking

of ways and means of raising the money to carry out God's plan. For yearly two years, I had been thinking, but God showed me the time had come for action. I was directed by God to believe that the necessary money was coming. I thought, 'God, how in the world will I get it?' I did not know. But the main thing of importance was that God was leading me to make a decision.

"Things began to happen in a hurry. I called the newspaper and announced I would preach a sermon the following morning entitled, 'What I would do if I had a Million Dollars.' I went to work on the sermon immediately, but the task was not difficult because I had been preparing that sermon for almost two years. The spirit of it was a part of me. Long before midnight I finished writing the sermon. I went to bed and slept with a feeling of confidence.

"Next morning I arose early, went into the bathroom, read the sermon, then knelt upon my knees and asked God to send to the service that morning, the person or circumstance He had picked who could supply the needed money.

"While I was praying, I again felt God's assurance that the money would be forthcoming. In my excitement, I walked out without my sermon, and did not discover the oversight until I was in the pulpit and about ready to begin delivering it. It was too late to go back for my notes, and what a blessing I couldn't go back. Instead, my own subconscious mind that God had prepared yielded the material I needed. When I arose to begin my sermon, I closed my eyes and spoke with all my heart and soul of the dream God had given me.

"I not only talked to my audience, I talked also to God. I told him and everyone there what I would do with a million dollars if that amount were placed in my hands. I described the plan I had in mind for organizing a great educational institution, where young people would learn to do practical things, and at the same time, develop their minds.

"When I had finished and sat down, a man slowly arose from his seat, about three rows from the rear, and made his way toward the pulpit. I wondered what he was going to do. He came into the pulpit, extended his hand, and said, 'Reverend, I liked your sermon. I believe you can do, everything you said you would, if you had a million dollars. To prove that I believe in you and your sermon, if you will come to my office tomorrow morning, I will give you the million dollars. My name is Phillip D. Armour."[2]

> "If you come to my office tomorrow morning, I will give you the million dollars."

Needless to say, Pastor Frank Gunsaulus was prompt at Armour's office the following morning. Phillip Armour was then the president of the great meat packing company on the south side of Chicago. That Monday morning, Frank Gunsaulus was given a check for one million dollars. In 1893, with the money given to him, Rev. Frank Gunsaulus founded what was to become the Armour Institute of

Technology, and later became the Illinois Institute of Technology. It was the very first school of its kind where students learned hands-on skills while at the same time developing their minds.[3] The entire technology training movement in America was founded by a minister with a God-given dream to change the way specialty education was done for the better!

> In training new church "specialists" for the 21st century, we invite you to join the NCS Support Team to help us make a difference.

While our calling and the training outcomes we have are different, our passion at New Church Specialties for the launch of New Church University is very similar to the passion that drove Frank Gunsaulus. We have a clear mission and plan *"to assist the starting and strengthening of NewStart, ReStart, ReFocusing and Parent churches worldwide."* If you have the means to do so and can assist us in training new church "specialists" for the 21st century, we invite you to join the NCS Support Team[4] and help us make a difference.

17

Qualified Coaches & Consultants

"Saul was accompanied by valiant men whose hearts God had touched... Whenever he saw a mighty or brave man, he took him into his service."
1 Samuel 10:26; 14:52

A key aspect of the vision God has given NCS is providing a qualified coach for every NewStart, ReStart, ReFocusing and Parent church leader who needs one. We also develop qualified church health consultants trained to serve our judicatory and denominational partners. Highly qualified coaches and consultants are needed by the hundreds and we have a great beginning. The training and personnel development task we face is immense. We have taken the US Army Corp of Engineers motto as our own: "The difficult we do immediately, the impossible takes a little longer!"

In clarifying the difference between coaching and consulting, for us a coach is someone who holds an individual leader accountable for the implementation of a Church Action Plan he or she has developed. A consultant is someone who works with a church, judicatory or denomination as they implement their strategies and plans. As we perfect our coaching and consulting processes, we are learning to clarify the nature, roles and expectations of the multiple parties involved in coaching and consulting agreements.

Characteristics of Effective Coaches

What are the characteristics of the people we seek to serve on our coaching and consulting team, both nationally and internationally? You must have *character*—your spirit must be right and your maturity developed. You must be *competent*—you must have developed specialty in your field. You must inspire *confidence*—what you say, do and teach must communicate to people a sense of assurance that you can be followed because you know what you are talking about.

We require all of our coaches and consultants who come through NCS coaches' training to use the excellent resource by Steve Ogne & Tom Nebel, "Empowering Leaders through Coaching."[1] In summary, these are the eight qualities we are looking for in identifying coaches who could potentially become nationally qualified with NCS.

1. Spiritual health and maturity
2. Good reputation with those who know them
3. Humility—being teachable and a life-long learner

4. Positive attitude
5. Passion to reach lost and broken people with the gospel
6. Expertise and growing competence in their field
7. Loyalty to *your judicatory* and to its coaching & consulting system in working with NCS
8. Availability and a commitment to coach, mentor or consult

Building A Strong Coaching Movement

We have learned the strength of any coaching movement is built on addressing three critical issues: recruitment, accountability and quality assurance. First of all, God is the one who ultimately leads recruitment and pulls the people of any genuine movement together. When Saul was selected as king over Israel and needed a team of leaders, the Bible explains that he was "accompanied by valiant men whose hearts *God* had touched" (1 Sam 10:26). God is ultimately the One who does the recruiting, not us. However, we must always be on the lookout for the best possible people to serve. "Whenever Saul saw a mighty or brave man, he took him into his service" (1 Sam 14:52).

The second issue that must be addressed for an effective coaching movement is accountability. As a team member, you must be loyal and committed both to the coaching and consulting system and to the judicatory or denomination in which the Lord has placed you. There are four parties in all of our coaching contracts: the coach, the person being coached, the denominational or project supervisor and the NCS Coaching office. Following every coaching appointment, our coaches are required by contract to send an e-mail to all parties involved in the agreement summarizing the good things happening, focus items agreed on, time of next scheduled appointment, etc. Without taking major supervisory time, the judicatory leader receives regular progress reports from a nationally qualified coach. This is another key feature that makes our partners "raving fans" of our coaching system.[2]

> We have learned the strength of any coaching movement requires addressing three critical issues: recruitment, accountability and quality assurance.

The third issue we must address is quality assurance. Our coaches must be good, and every party involved in the coaching agreement must be a "raving fan" of the coaching being delivered. NCS coaching comes with a full satisfaction guarantee to our partners, which requires us to be *very* diligent in our national qualification process.

We now provide Coaching Level 1 & Level 2 training with a graduated process of moving from Coach-In-Training to Associate Coach to Senior Coach status. We also provide opportunities for on-going coaching skill development.

As New Church Specialties has developed, so has the coaching "specialties" NCS offers. We are developing

NewStart coaches, ReStart coaches and ReFocusing coaches. We are also seeing Parent church and church health consultants being raised up to serve the church.

Building Coaching Credibility

Within judicatories and denominational families, the ability of coaches and consultants to be effective requires growing levels of credibility. How is this credibility built? *Empowering Leaders through Coaching* has done a great job identifying the four sources of building credibility.[3] At NCS, we use and teach these to all NCS team members. Let me summarize the four sources of coaching or consulting credibility.

The first source is **positional credibility**. If you are a judicatory leader, we have learned that for you to lead an effective movement, you must be truly helpful, not just important. Beyond being a results person, you must become a *resource* person. People under your leadership must feel that when you connect with them by phone or meet them in person, it is for genuine encouragement, not just a "checkup." We have observed that some judicatory leaders do not connect with the people they lead, while others are great *resourcers* and encouragers. If you complete the coaching qualification process with NCS, you may have some beginning credibility through this "position." One thing is certain, however; positional credibility alone cannot sustain a healthy leadership or coaching relationship.

The second source is **expertise credibility**. This may

come because you have NewStart, ReStart, ReFocusing or Parent church experience. You may be skilled in strategic planning in the business world and have a real heart for the church. If you are recognized with experience, knowledge and expertise in your field, you are immediately perceived as helpful. With personal experience, you can point out possible mistakes people may make, thus helping them with trial and error learning. However, have you ever met someone who was very skilled or knowledgeable, yet you did not like them or want to listen to them? So, while vitally important to develop, expertise authority by itself is not sufficient for sustaining long-term coaching or consulting relationships.

The third source is **spiritual credibility**. Spiritual authority (or credibility) is given by God alone, but when present it is recognized by others. It is usually linked closely with the development of spiritual discernment. Spiritual authority develops through the long-term practice of spiritual disciplines such as prayer, frugality, sacrifice, submission, scripture memory, worship, solitude, study and service. Paul described it as having a ministry "not with wise and persuasive words but in demonstration of the Spirit's power, so that your faith does not rest on men's wisdom but on God's power" (1 Cor 2:4-5). After you work with someone for awhile, you sense whether or not they have been with Jesus (Acts 4:13). While this is the most subjective source of credibility, when it is developed and is present in your life, it will multiply your coaching/ consulting effectiveness greatly.

The fourth source is **relational credibility.** This is the result of you taking time to develop a personal relationship of trust with the leader with whom you are working. Relational authority is much more quickly established when you are perceived as having one or more other sources of credibility. Of the four, relational credibility is the most important in sustaining a coaching and consulting relationship. As a coach or consultant, you need to understand the sources of your own credibility. Every coach or consultant begins with one or more of them. If you develop multiple sources of coaching credibility, this will obviously help you serve with greater effectiveness. If you develop and demonstrate competence in your particular field of expertise, you can gain some "positional credibility" by becoming a nationally qualified coach or consultant. The development of expertise, spiritual, and relational credibility is something great coaches continue to pursue.

Becoming a Coach

Our objective is to multiply and provide high-quality coaching and consulting to local church, judicatory and denominational partners. The task is great and the need for NewStart, ReStart, ReFocusing and Parent church coaches is huge. The development of hundreds of qualified coaches will require a commitment to the continued development of a learning organization environment within judicatories and denominational families. Have you felt a calling to multiply your ministry? Do the people around you affirm your coaching/mentoring skills? Have you developed expertise as a NewStart, ReStart, ReFocusing or Parent church leader? As a lay leader, has God gifted you with strategic planning skills that you may be able to use for the growth of the Kingdom? If the answer is yes, God may be leading you to seek training, become a qualfied coach or consultant and invest your life in assisting your judicatory, denomination or fellowship.

Because of our commitment to interdependent relationships in launching church health and church multiplication movements, NCS does not train independent coaches or consultants. To enter the coaching process, you must first secure the approval of the judicatory leader or person to whom you are spiritually accountable. For more information on the process of becoming nationally qualfied, we encourage you to first contact your judicatory or denomination and then visit NCS on the Web under the coaching or consulting section. We turn now to the last source of movement fuel, the development of a worldwide vision and commitment.

> Because of our commitment to interdependent relationships, NCS does not train independent coaches or consultants.

18

A Worldwide Vision & Commitment

"As the time approached for Jesus to be taken up to heaven, He resolutely set out for Jerusalem."
Luke 9:51

All kinds of diversions came up along the way for our Lord as He traveled to Jerusalem, headed toward the cross. When Jesus laid out His mission, which included suffering and death, Peter "took Him aside and began to rebuke Him. 'Never, Lord!' he said. 'This shall never happen to you!'" (Matt 16:22) Jesus was severe in His response. "Get behind me, Satan! You are a stumbling block to me; you do not have in mind the things of God, but the things of men" (Matt 16:23). Jesus refused to be distracted.

An ancient adage says, "If you want to defeat them…distract them." All during His ministry, Jesus had numerous opportunities to lose His focus. These opportunities usually related to the talents and skills Jesus had. With His power and ability, Jesus could have done many things differently than He did. He could have healed a lot more sick people, taken the time to write some incredible books, or traveled much more widely. But Jesus did not choose any of these options. He was resolute, focused, and through His obedience to the Father, He was powerfully effective.

Loving the Church — Worldwide

What is the spirit that surrounds your life as a Christian? More important than any "specialty" we may have, any coaching, training or competence in our area of expertise, is the spirit that surrounds our lives. What is the atmosphere that people sense when they talk to you? Every person gives attention, consciously or unconsciously to some kind of vision, which then creates an atmosphere.

We believe the spirit and atmosphere that makes any church health and church multiplication movement great is our spirit of love for the church. This spirit of love must ooze out of us all the time. It is the heart of God. It is also what gives us the hearts of men and women who lead the church. Christians must be challenged to "love the church and give themselves up for her, just like Jesus did...so that she may be presented to Him without spot or wrinkle, but holy and blameless" (Eph 5:25-27).

Our love for the church must be as broad as that of Jesus — **it must be worldwide**. Paul describes the new church in Thessalonica, "The Lord's message rang out from you not only in Macedonia and Achaia — your faith in God *has become known everywhere*." What a tremendous testimony about the spirit of this new church!

What would happen if this became the personal

commitment of every church? We are never called to build our own kingdom. Jesus taught us to pray, "thy kingdom come, thy will be done" (Matt 6:10). Your commitment to develop your local congregation into a worldwide, globally focused church is the clear vision of the New Testament.

The vision of God in the Old Testament was to use Israel to bring salvation to the entire world. Numerous scripture passages teach this.[1] Jesus' vision for His disciples was worldwide. He clearly has a global vision for every Christian and every congregation today.

> Love for the church is the heart of God. It is also what gives us the heart of men and women who lead the church.

He challenges us, "Go and make disciples of all nations..." (Matt 28:19). This is not a mandate just for denominational mission agencies or mission organizations. This is our mission, directly from Jesus Himself, given as a mandate to every Christian and every local church.

As you and I seek God's vision for us, we must make sure it is both biblical and global. To be the first (biblical), it must be the second (global).

We have seen over and over again that a biblical and global church vision always begins in the heart and attitude of the pastor and leadership team.

As biblical Christians, our thinking must be the same as that of our Lord–with global objectives always in mind. With Jesus Christ as our leader, God's plan includes our entire planet, and one day it will happen.

"The kingdoms of this world shall become the kingdoms of our Lord and of His Christ and He will reign forever and ever" (Rev 11:15). Because this is God's plan for the world, there is a global mission for every church.

When Should World Mission Support Begin?

In many new and existing churches across North America, however, the question is often raised, "Why should we support our denominational missions' efforts? We need money for our ministry here at home. We are not strong enough to give money away. Now is not the time to be concerned about the global call of Christianity. We will be committed to that in the future, just not now."

This is a common attitude found these days throughout the church. It is not a new attitude. This kind of thinking has been around for a long time. I want to suggest that this issue is not just a monetary one, it is a theological one. It again comes down to our basic beliefs about the church. *Our answer is directly related to our doctrine of ecclesiology.* What do we believe about the nature, mission and vision of Christ's church?

What does Jesus think about this issue? Does He address it in the Scriptures? No serious Christian questions whether or not we should be committed to reaching the entire world with the good news of the gospel. In the Great Commission, our Lord makes very clear, "Go and make disciples of all nations" (Matt 28:19). The question is, *when* does our mission become global? When does Jesus expect us to be committed globally? In the second year, the fourth year, or the sixth year after we come to Christ?

When does Jesus expect *our church* to be committed to being a globally-minded church? When should we make a commitment to begin building global Christians? In the second year, the fourth year, or the sixth year after our church is started? I want to suggest that if the DNA for building global Christians is not put into a Christian from day one, or is not put into a local church from day one, we are discipling a Christian and building a church that is in disobedience to the mission and vision of Jesus. This is not to say that we expect people who are spiritually less than six months old to be fully committed and take their two-week vacation to go on mission trips. What we are talking about here is the DNA of the church's vision and the strategic thinking of the church's leadership.

Becoming a Global Christian

If I truly seek to have the heart of Jesus, I will seek to think the way He thinks, not just about myself and my ministry, but about the world. I will seek to feel what He feels, to cry over what He cries over, to laugh about what He laughs about, to see what He sees, every day I live. I will not just sing songs in worship services about honoring Him in all I do. I will seek to prove my faith and commitment to the vision of Jesus with action (Jam 2:18).

It is the vision of Jesus that calls me to wake up every day and think about the world. All too often the world is out of our vision as Christians; we do not regularly think about it. God sees the world, He thinks about the world, 24 hours a day, seven days a week. As global Christians, we should too. What follows is a listing of both countries and world areas, organized into nine regions to remind every reader of the world Jesus loves. We encourage you to take a moment and read the name of each country of the world out loud.

North America: (2)

Canada	United States of America

Mexico & Central America: (8)

Belize	Guatemala	Nicaragua
Costa Rica	Honduras	Panama
El Salvador	Mexico	

Caribbean: (24)

Anguilla	Dominica	Puerto Rico
Antigua & Barbuda	Dominican Republic	Trinidad & Tobago
Aruba	French West Indies	Turks & Calcos
The Bahamas	Grenada	St. Kitts & Nevis
Barbados	Haiti	St. Lucia
Bermuda	Jamaica	St. Vincent &
British Virgin Islands	Montserrat	the Grenadines
Cayman Islands	Netherlands Antilles	Virgin Islands
Cuba		

South America: (13)

Argentina	Ecuador	Peru
Bolivia	French Guiana	Suriname
Brazil	Guyana	Uruguay
Colombia	Paraguay	Venezuela
Chile		

Africa: (52)

Algeria
Angola
Azores
Benin
Botswana
Burkina Faso
Burundi
Cameroon
Cape Verde Islands
Central African Rep.
Chad
Comoros
Congo (Brazzaville)
Congo (Kinshasa)
Cote d'Ivoire
Djibouti
Equatorial Guinea
Eritrea

Ethiopia
Gabon
The Gambia
Ghana
Guinea
Guinea-Bissau
Kenya
Lesotho
Liberia
Libya
Madagascar
Malawi
Mali
Mauritania
Morocco
Mozambique
Namibia
Niger

Nigeria
Rwanda
Sao Tome/Principe
Senegal
Seychelles
Sierra Leone
Somalia
South Africa
Sudan
Swaziland
Tanzania
Togo
Tunisia
Uganda
Zambia
Zimbabwe

Europe: (38)

Albania
Andorra
Austria
Belgium
Bosnia & Herzegovina
Bulgaria
Croatia
Czech Republic
Denmark, Greenland
    & the Faroe Islands
Estonia
Finland
France

Germany
Greece
Hungary
Iceland
Ireland
Italy
Latvia
Lithuania
Luxembourg
Macedonia
Malta
Moldava
Monaco

Netherlands
Norway
Poland
Portugal
Romania
Serbia/Montenegro
Slovak Republic
Slovenia
Spain
Sweden
Switzerland
United Kingdom
    & Gibralter

Middle East: (16)

Bahrain	Jordan	Saudi Arabia
Cyprus	Kuwait	Syria
Egypt	Lebanon	Turkey
Iran	Oman	United Arab Emirates
Iraq	Qatar	Yemen
Israel, the West Bank & Gaza		

Central Asia: (20)

Afghanistan	Georgia	Nepal
Armenia	India	Pakistan
Azerbaijan	Kazakhstan	Russia
Bangladesh	Kyrgyz Republic	Sri Lanka
Belarus	Maldives	Tajikistan
Bhutan	Mauritius	Turkmenistan
Burma (Myanmar)	Mongolia	

East Asia & Oceania: (33)

Australia	Laos	Philippines
Brunei	Macau	Samoa
Cambodia	Malaysia	Singapore
China	Marshall Islands	Solomon Islands
East Timor	Micronesia	South Korea
Fiji	Nauru	Taiwan
French Polynesia	New Caledonia	Thailand
Hong Kong	New Zealand	Tonga
Indonesia	North Korea	Tuvalu
Japan	Palau	Vanuatu
Kiribati	Papua New Guinea	Vietnam

We encourage you to study the countries of the world, become familiar with them, think and pray about them, and ask God to give you a heart for reaching each one of them with the gospel. Depending on how we count territories and dependencies of other nations, there are approximately 206 countries and world areas. God has an incredible desire to extend His love to every one of the 6½ billion persons who live in them. "God so loved **the world** that He gave His one and only Son…" (John 3:16).

If the World Were 100 People

Sometimes the idea of understanding these 6½ billion people in the world can be a bit overwhelming for some people. How can we better get our minds and hearts to clearly see and feel what Jesus feels every day when He looks at the world? It may be easier for us to develop a clearer understanding if we were to use the analogy of shrinking the entire world into a village of 100 people. All of us can get our minds around that. If the entire world were 100 people in a village, the following would be a fairly accurate description of it:

- 61 would be Asian
- 13 would be African
- 12 would be European
- 8 would be South American
- 6 would be North American
- 30 would be children and 70 would be adults
- 52 would be women and 48 would be men
- 1 would have AIDS
- 17 would speak Chinese, 9 would speak English, 8 would speak Hindi, 6 would speak Spanish and 60 would speak something else

- 20 would be undernourished and 1 dying of starvation
- 1 would have a college education, 2 would have a computer, 4 would have access to the internet and 14 would be unable to read nor write
- 6 people would own 59% of the world's wealth and they would all live in the United States
- the poorest 20 people would share 2% of the wealth
- 20 people would live in fear of attack, rape, bombardment or land mines
- 33 would be Christian
- 19 would be Muslim
- 13 would be Hindu
- 6 would be Buddhist
- 5 would worship spirits in the trees, rocks, rivers, etc.
- 24 would worship something else or nothing

Most denominational and fellowship families have developed a significant group of people who are truly global Christians. When it comes to the world, they see what Jesus sees, consistently. They have reordered their lives accordingly. The challenge we face is that we need literally millions more just like them. We need every pastor to be a global Christian. We need every church lay leader, every youth leader, and every church planter to get and keep the big picture of the world. Because we follow Christ, our mission is worldwide from the first day we come to Christ and the first day we plant a new church.

With this established, denominational and judicatory leaders must be patient with new Christians and new churches as they mature. Proper policies and procedures should be clearly agreed on and established that will assist new churches in becoming an active part of the missionary support system of their denominational or fellowship family.

We have found that if the relationship is strong between the local congregation, the planter and the judicatory, mission support naturally follows as the new church and new Christians mature.

Embracing a Worldwide Vision

We can only achieve our global objectives as Christians if we keep planting strong, healthy new churches. They must be planted in every country and culture of the world. Churches that are planted in affluent areas must understand Paul's clear teaching on giving (2 Cor 8-9) and God's concern for the poor. Jesus was born poor, identified with the poor and ministered to them.[2] Most North American church plants are very wealthy compared to the rest of the world. Getting involved in inner-city ministries and participating in mission trips to developing countries are two ways we can help new Christians coming to the church to more clearly see the world and its needs from God's perspective.

What is it that you think about every day? What atmosphere surrounds your life? What has captured your heart? Where do you invest most of your time and money? I hope God will use this book as a reminder for you to more regularly think the way He thinks about the world and the multiplication of healthy churches worldwide. The world will never believe unless they hear, and they will never hear unless someone preaches to them and this preaching will not happen unless someone is trained and sent (Rom 10:14-15) to train others (2 Tim 2:2).

Whether you are in a NewStart, ReStart, ReFocusing or Parent church, the vision from heaven for all of us is the same. God calls us to a worldwide commitment. As Christians, we cannot be disobedient to His vision (Acts 26:19). Within your denomination, judicatory or fellowship, will you commit today to be part of the sending team about whom the scriptures speak, "how beautiful are the feet of those who bring good news!"? (Rom 10:15)

What is God saying to you at this moment? What would He have you adjust in your thinking, your speaking or your living as it concerns His global mandate? If your heart is responsive, His mission has already begun to be fulfilled where you live! Before you put down this book, make a renewed commitment to partner wholeheartedly with other like-minded Christians in God's church where He has placed you. When we as Christ-followers lock arms together in agenda harmony and share a worldwide vision, we have our Lord's promise that then "the entire world will know!" (John 17:23).

Our Mission and Ministry Description

Mission: "To assist the starting and strengthening of NewStart, ReStart, ReFocusing and Parent churches worldwide."

Ministry Description: "New Church Specialties is a non-profit organization specializing in coaching pastors and church planters, consulting judicatories and denominations, and providing NewStart, ReStart, ReFocusing and Parent church education and training through New Church University. We exist to serve the mission and ministry of the church."

About the Author

Dr. Larry McKain is the founder and Executive Director of New Church Specialties, a non-profit organization currently with a paid staff of thirty-six and seven offices across the United States. He has written the curriculum and launched a training and coaching system for church leaders called New Church University, which has also been translated into Spanish. In the past four years, he has spoken to over 35,000 people and trained 3,000 church leaders through New Church University.

He is a graduate of Mid-America Nazarene University, Nazarene Theological Seminary, and has an earned doctorate from Fuller Seminary. He has personally planted four churches and has coached and influenced the starting of hundreds of new churches across the U.S. & Canada. His "Insights" e-mail goes out to 8,200 church leaders each week. To date, New Church Specialties has served a total of 21 different denominations.

Larry and his wife, Denise, are the parents of two children, Sarah & Wesley. The McKains make their home in Kansas City, Missouri.

"Preferred Training Provider" for Denominations

New Church Specialties has become the "preferred provider" for training church planters and Parent church leaders in the 1,700 congregations of the Wesleyan denomination, as well as the 5,000 churches of the Nazarene denomination in the United States and Canada. In making the announcement, Jerry Pence, now General Superintendent for the Wesleyan Church, stated, "NCS' New Church University has proven to be an especially effective, denominationally-friendly program, worthy of special consideration by Wesleyan church planting sponsors."

The Wesleyan Evangelism & Church Growth Department now provides both New Church University scholarships and some coaching scholarships to Wesleyan planters who complete a qualified Assessment, attend New Church University and hire a qualified coach. Some scholarship funds are also now available for Wesleyan Senior Pastors who want to attend the New Church University Parent Church Track for learning how to Parent or Sponsor a new church. The General Department of Evangelism & Church Growth of the Wesleyan Church is also now encouraging all Wesleyan Districts to consider a judicatory partnership with NCS.

Dr. Tom Nees of the Church of the Nazarene has also chosen to use NCS training for the whole denomination and in his decision stated, "New Church Specialties is helping the Church of the Nazarene develop missional leaders and missional churches. Because of their professional and effective training, we have contracted with NCS to be the 'preferred provider' of training for the development of church action plans. I encourage all of our districts and churches to partner with NCS and utilize their services." We are grateful for our partnership with the Wesleyan and Nazarene denominations and anticipate partnership with other denominational families will emerge in the future.

Benefits of NCS Partnership

A Partner Judicatory is a judicatory that has a working, contractual relationship with NCS. NCS Partner benefits keep on expanding as NCS continues to develop. The following is a basic list of benefits.

1. The trial and error learning, as well as "success" learning that NCS is collecting and capturing from our work with all our NCS Partners.

2. The learning, networking and training provided through New Church University.

3. A personal and contextualized policy & procedures manual for NewStart, ReStart, ReFocusing & Parent churches.

4. Motivation & faith building to assist in launching your judicatory movement.

5. Development of a NewStart, ReStart, ReFocusing & Parent church education process & competency standards for your judicatory.

6. Access to and help through the NCS recruiting and tracking process for future church planters.

7. Judicatory "on-site" consulting, chosen from the NCS list of services. Partner contracts vary, depending on the amount of consulting time and services needed by the judicatory.

8. Phone calls and e-mails to all NCS offices for the entire length of the contract period, from designated persons in the judicatory.

9. Scholarships to New Church University for pastors from

partner judicatories and additional scholarships for pastors whose judicatories sponsor an NCU.

10. Opportunity to sponsor a national New Church University event at a site within your judicatory—subject to availability.

11. Discounts available from NCS Church Health for church health surveys performed for congregations located in Partner Judicatories.

12. Access to NCS Resources that continue to be developed.

13. Access to D.S. Direct[3] and all of the resources it contains for Denominational Supervisors (judicatory leaders) to use.

14. Access to the NCS Assessment process for training your own judicatory to do church leader assessments. We also offer Church Health Consultant & Local Church Assessment Training.

15. Provide to our Partner Judicatories an "Insights" e-mail update annually, to ensure church leaders within the judicatory are receiving NCS Insights.

16. A full satisfaction, money-back guarantee

How NCS Is Financed

From the beginning, the NCS development strategy has been a combination of individual and organizational contributions, as well as income from fees for service rendered. NCS Support Team members who share the vision of NCS provide about 20% of our operating capital each year. The other 80% of our income comes from coaching and consulting fees,

NCU tuition and other services we render.

In reality, it is the top 20% from NCS Support Team contributions that allows the other 80% of our ministry services to be delivered. Historically, every $1 an individual, organization or church contributes to NCS is leveraged with another $4 of ministry services we are then able to provide.

Over the next 25 years, the vision of NCS is to assist our partners in training 30,000 church leaders, assist in starting 10,000 new churches, assist 5,000 churches to refocus their ministries, assist 5,000 churches to parent a new church and help train 500 qualified coaches. Beyond our fees for service, our vision is to raise $15 million to fund the achievement of what we believe God is calling us to do both in North America and throughout the world. We anticipate this will assist our partners with two million new people being led to Christ and discipled through regular involvement in their churches.

In this process, our Support Team, who has a heart for our work, allows us to maintain our high commitment to be a genuine not-for-profit organization. The Senior Staff of NCS regularly give away large amounts of both donated services and New Church University scholarships each year. Beyond the NCS budget, over the past four years, that total has been **$374,457** for which we praise God!

Because of the NCS Support Team, NCS has been able to provide hundreds of donated coaching and consulting hours to individuals and churches unable to fully pay for our services.

As God continues to provide, we are committed to continue serving the church by giving away tens of thousands of dollars in both scholarships and other donated services in the years to come. Our commitment is to keep costs as fair as possible to our partners, while continuing each year to improve the service we provide.

Our Commitment to Donors

We believe that the way an organization handles its finances is a reflection of its integrity in every other area. We have, therefore, established clear guidelines for the way NCS resources are raised and used. Here are the commitments NCS has made in our ministry to our Support Team.

1. The ministry of NCS belongs to God. It seems the Lord has sovereignly chosen to place His hand of approval on us. We know He gives and He sometimes takes away (Job 1:21). If He ever closes the door on our work, we will accept His leading. Until then, we will devote all of our energies to the worldwide mission He has given us.

2. The first priority is the local church. We ask you not to support NCS until your obligations to your local church have been met. We believe the local church is God's plan and vehicle for bringing salvation to the world.

3. Every gift, sacrificially given. We consider every contribution we receive from you as a gift from God, sent through loving people who have sacrificed to make the gift possible. We will never take our financial support for granted, nor ever cease to be deeply grateful for every dollar the Lord entrusts to us.

4. Every gift, strategically leveraged. For every dollar you donate, NCS pledges to multiply it through scholarships, donated work and fees for service. In the past two years, the ratio has been 20% - 80%. In other words, for every $1 donated, NCS has matched it in ministry with $4. When scholarships and donated services are added, the leveraged amount is increased even more.

5. Operating with open books. We will be completely open about NCS finances. We publish an annual report that declares all NCS income and expenses which is available to you. Our 990's are also available upon request. We undergo regular auditing from an outside CPA firm (2 Cor 8:21).

6. A commitment to excellence, not extravagance. Our obligation is to spend monies given sacrificially in a conservative and wise manner. Every dollar you give will be stretched as far as possible, keeping necessary overhead lean and efficient, while maintaining ministry excellence.

7. Our attitude during lean times. One of the ways we can discern the Lord's will regarding the continuation of our work is through the support He sends (or doesn't send) from His people. Therefore, during lean times we will make our obligations known to you—but never manipulate you in seeking contributions. We will never resort to what we consider to be disrespectful methods of fund-raising, even when our needs are serious.

8. Using the money of vendors. When we make a purchase, we will pay the invoice within 30 days, if possible. We do not intend to use the money of our vendors.

9. Donor and mailing list privacy. We will never sell or rent our contacts or mailing list to those wishing to use the names and addresses of our donors, clients or partners. We will always maintain the tightest security on the information you give us.

10. Keeping our donors informed. In maintaining our accountability to you, we will keep you informed of the ministry progress of NCS. We believe you can discern the will of God regarding your stewardship as long as we provide you with the right information.

11. We will pray for you. The Bible says if you share financially with us, that is our obligation to you. We take the Great Commission of Jesus (Matt 28:18-20) very seriously and understand the gift of giving is vital to its fulfillment (Rom 12:8).

As a member of the NCS Support Team, we pledge to live before you with integrity in all of our financial matters. Thank you for the trust you have placed in us.

Building Raving Fans — Serving with Excellence

We want to thank you for purchasing *Falling in Love with the Church,* which outlines the process of building agenda harmony for church health and church multiplication movements. We hope this has given you some insight about the strategies and philosophy behind what we do at New Church Specialties. Ken Blanchard, author of the *One Minute Manager*, has written a book entitled *Raving Fans — A Revolutionary Approach to Customer Service*. It is not a religious book but the application to what we are doing is very powerful. From the beginning, NCS has been guided by these three simple principles. A summary of Blanchard's three secrets to developing "raving fans" that we follow is below.

1. Decide on a very clear vision. Have a very clear picture, a clear vision of the ideal. The ideal is the clear future you envision. Make sure this ideal is centered on the people you serve.

2. Discover what the people you are serving need. Discover what the people you serve want and need, and then fill in the gaps from your vision. You will only discover what the people you serve want in small nuggets. Everyone you meet has a slightly different focus and need. Fit that into your own vision. If you meet people's needs, you will never lack opportunities for ministry. For those people you cannot satisfy, quickly learn to emotionally let them go.

3. Discover what the people you are serving need — deliver plus one percent! After you discover what the people you serve want and need, then deliver, plus one percent. The rule of one percent is to keep on consistently improving what you do, one percent at a time. Go the extra mile in your service, and you will never lack for a crowd of "raving fans."[4]

At New Church Specialties, we are committed to providing you with the very best customer service we possibly can. That is our commitment to every Denominational and Judicatory Partner and NewStart, ReStart, ReFocusing and Parent church leader with whom we work. If we need to improve in some way, please tell us. If we do a great job, please tell someone else! We really do want you a "raving fan." Thank you for the privilege and opportunity of serving you.

Contact Information:
NCS on the Web: www.NewChurchSpecialties.org
NCS Main Office — Kansas City, MO:
New Church Specialties
6502 NW Mil-Mar Dr.
Kansas City, MO 64151

Phone: 816-746-6468
Fax: 816-746-6444
E-Mail: KCOffice@NewChurchSpecialties.org

NCS Services Now Available

In the NCS Consultant Training Process, we train our Senior Coaches & Consultants to deliver the following services to our judicatory partners, denominational partners and local churches. We will continue to add new "specialties" in our on-going development.

Assessment
1. Complete Local Church Assessments
2. Church Health, Life-Cycle and other Survey Tools
3. Church Planter Assessments

Training
4. Church Leader Assessment Training
5. New Church University Events (national & regional)
6. 1 & 2 Day NCS Contextualized Seminars (Church Planting, ReFocusing, Parenting, Coaching, Church Health, etc.)

Coaching & Consulting
7. Parent & Sponsor Church Coaching/Consulting
8. NewStart & ReStart Coaching
9. ReFocusing Coaching
10. Leading Coaching Clusters
11. Local Church Strategic Planning
12. Church Closure & ReStart Consulting
13. ReLocation & ReLaunch Consulting
14. Spiritual "ReFocusing" Week-Ends
15. Church Planter Recruitment System Development
16. Judicatory Church Planter Tracking System

Notes & Credits

Introduction
[1]While we often refer to the church and the Kingdom of God inter-changeably, they are uniquely different. The church is referred to in the New Testament as a divine-human creation of God, the incarnation of Jesus today and is an organized community of faith. (See W. T. Purkiser, Richard S. Taylor, *God, Man & Salvation — A Biblical Theology* (Kansas City, MO: Beacon Hill Press, 1977) pp 597-623.

[2]The church of Jesus Christ is much too complex, diverse and expansive for us to seek an organized, structural unity. By spiritual unity we mean the attitude which surrounds our Christian activity should not emphasize the differences among denominational families, but rather emphasize our common mission in introducing people to Jesus and making disciples who follow Him throughout the world. We believe this can be done without blurring denominational distinctives or heritage. Unity can be achieved without uniformity.

Chapter 1
[1]Taken from *The Bride* by Charles R. Swindoll. Copyright © 1994 by Charles R. Swindoll. Used by permission of The Zondervan Corporation, p 9.

Chapter 2
[1]W.T. Purkiser, Richard S. Taylor & Willard H. Taylor, *God, Man & Salvation – A Biblical Theology,* p 565.

[2]At New Church University, we train church leaders to identify the steps of obedience they envision people taking in the disciple-making process and build a ministry flow chart (see page 121).

[3]Taken from *Purpose-Driven® Church*, The by Rick Warren. Copyright © 1995 by Rick Warren. Used by permission of the Zondervan Corporation, p 17.

[4]Taken from *Fresh Wind, Fresh Fire* by Jim Cymbala; Dean Merrill. Copyright © 1997 by Jim Cymbala. Used by permission of the Zondervan Corporation, p 121.

[5]Christian Schwarz, *Natural Church Development* (Carol Stream, IL: ChurchSmart Resources, 1996) For information about how NCS integrates NCD with Church Assessments and NCU Church Action Plans, contact any one of our NCS Senior Consultants or NCS Offices.

Chapter 4
[1]The church is a sacramental community, where Christ comes into the presence of a people (see *God, Man & Salvation*, pp 575-596). The scope of this book does not allow us to address this issue in depth but we hope many will want to study further on the subject.

[2]W.T. Purkiser, Richard S. Taylor & Willard H. Taylor, *God, Man & Salvation – A Biblical Theology*, p 564.

Chapter 5
[1]Bill Sullivan, *Churches Starting Churches* (Kansas City, MO: Nazarene Publishing House, 2001) p 8.

[2]Stephen R. Covey, *The Seven Habits of Highly Effective People* (New York, NY: Simon & Schuster, 1989) p 9.

[3]John Dawson, *Taking Your Cities For God* (Lake Mary, FL: Creation House Publishers, 1989) p 91.

Chapter 6
[1]For more information on board renewal weekends or church strategic planning, contact the NCS Main Office: KCOffice@NewChurch Specialties.org or call (816) 746-6468.

Chapter 7
[1]Covey, *The Seven Habits of Highly Effective People*, p 95.

[2]NCU National Team, *New Church Blueprints* (Kansas City, MO: NCS Publishing, 2004), pp 3-4. *New Church Blueprints* is an evergreen notebook of resources that continues to be changed quarterly through feedback from New Church University Training events and updated annually.

[3]We have identified 12 major components in the NCU Parent Church training track. See NCS on the Web (www.NewChurchSpecialties.org) for more information.

[4]Another helpful tool is part three of *The Purpose-Driven Church* by Rick Warren, pages 155-203.

[5]See page 144 of the *Purpose Driven Church* for this example.

[6]For information on TellStart, visit www.TellStart.com or e-mail Phil at phil@tellstart.com.

[7]Out of the eight health characteristics in the NCD Church Health analysis we use, the minimum factor is the lowest score identified.

Chapter 8
[1]For information on NCS Behavioral Interviewing assessment, you may contact Lonnie via e-mail at LBullock@NewChurchSpecialtie s.org.

Chapter 9
[1]Bill Sullivan, *Starting Strong New Churches* (Kansas City, MO: Beacon Hill Press, 1997) p 49.

Chapter 10
[1]For congregations who desire it, NCS now offers a complete church assessment. This includes: 1) Life-Cycle Determination, 2) Church Health Evaluation & Report, 3) Statistical Review, 4) Core Values Audit, 5) Governing Board Audit, 6) Leadership Assessment and 7) On-site visit with an NCS Senior Consultant. For more information, contact Lonnie via e-mail: LBullock@NewChurchSpecialties.org.

[2]Kelly A. Fryer, *Reclaiming the "L" Word – Renewing the Church from Its Lutheran Core* (Minneapolis, MN: Augsburg Fortress, 2003) p 87.

[3]We encourage every church beginning the ReFocusing process to first do an NCD Church Health Evaluation. This can be ordered by contacting the NCS Church Health Office at (480) 659-2547. For a complete church assessment, see the information on note 1 above.

Chapter 11
[1]God has taken care of Pastor Ron. Today Ron Thornton pastors a strong church in Newton, Kansas.

[2]A home church fellowship is a church that has chosen the path of corporate sanctification and given their assets up for the multiplication of the Christian movement. The organization of a home church fellowship varies widely, depending on the particular judicatory polity. They continue to worship together as they can, care for each other and share their resources with the wider church. Because of their financial capabilities, they are usually led by a lay leader or lay pastor.

Chapter 12
[1]Edwin McManus, *The Unstoppable Force* (Loveland, CO: Group Publishing, 2001) p 67.

[2]"Insights" is an NCS electronic resource published weekly and sent via e-mail currently to over 8,200 church leaders from dozens of denominations. Free registration is available at NCS on the Web. (www.NewChurchSpecialties.org).

[3]Charles R. Ridley, *How To Select Church Planters* (Pasadena, CA: Fuller Evangelistic Association, 1988). This self-study manual is the result of extensive field research I participated in as a planter during the mid 1980's. Dr. Ridley's results have become the "standard" for screening, interviewing and evaluating church planters.

[4]Malcolm Gladwell, *The Tipping Point* (Boston, MA: Little, Brown and Company, 2002).

Chapter 14

[1]We highly encourage church leaders interested in learning how to effectively parent to purchase copies of The Ripple Church, written by NCS Senior Consultant Phil Stevenson. To do so, visit the NCS Resources section of NCS on the Web. (www.NewChurchSpecialties.org).

Chapter 15

[1]Claude Payne & Hamilton Beazley, *Reclaiming the Great Commission* (San Francisco, CA: Jossey-Bass, 2001).

[2]While several theologians agree with this interpretation, because of the multiplicity of theological positions on spiritual gifts held by great Christian thinkers, our thoughts here are offered only as our opinion, not as a dogmatic spiritual position.

Chapter 16

[1]We offer very consistent advice to judicatories, denominational leaders and fellowships who desire long-term systemic change and the transformation of their judicatory "climate" and culture. You should move past trying by investing in building a quality training system and do not give up on your training system until it begins producing the results you desire. There is no quick fix. Solid training systems produce long-term results.

[2]Napoleon Hill, *Think and Grow Rich* (Cleveland, OH: Ralston Publishing Co., 1937), pp. 137-139, abridged.

[3]Illinois Institute of Technology is still in existence today and thriving. To read a brief history of IIT and see where this University is today, go to: http://www.iit.edu/about/history.html.

[4]For more information about supporting the ministry of New Church Specialties, call the NCS Main Office (816) 746-6468.

Chapter 17

[1]Steven Ogne & Thomas Nebel, *Empowering Leaders through Coaching*, (Carol Stream, IL: ChurchSmart Resources, 1995)

[2]NCS currently has 59 nationally qualified coaches. For more information about securing a coach or becoming a coach, contact our National Coaching Director, Tim Gates via e-mail: TGates@NewChurchSpecialties. org.

[3]Ogne & Nebel, pp 3-1 through 3-5.

Chapter 18

[1]Gen 12:3; Psa 2:8; 19:4, 22:27, 65:5, 67:7, 98:2-3; Isa 45:22, 49:6, 52:10, Jonah 4:11; Micah 5:4 is just a beginning sample of scriptures.

[2]Many passages explain God's heart for the poor and weak: Psa 41:1; Pro 19:17; Isa 10:1-2; Amos 8:4-7; Luke 4:18-19, 7:20-23; Jam 1:27. The New Testament reveals that many early Christians were poor and God expected the church to treat them properly (1 Cor 1:26-29; Jam 2:1-9)

Information about NCS

[1]D.S. Direct is a website designed by and for denominational supervisors who have become NCS Partners. Entry to the site is located at NCS on the Web. Access requires both the entry of the partner user name and password.

[2]Ken Blanchard, *Building Raving Fans – A Revolutionary Approach to Customer Service* (New York, NY: William Morrow & Co., 1993)

Subject Index

Scripture Index